MY EMPTY NEST

WAS SUPPOSED TO HAVE

TWO BIRDS

To my sweet friend,
Rhian
From:
Mike

My Empty Nest

WAS SUPPOSED TO HAVE

TWO BIRDS

A Recovery Journey Following Suicide

McKAY MOORE SOHLBERG

LUMINARE PRESS

WWW.LUMINAREPRESS.COM

Luminare Press
442 Charnelton St.
Eugene, OR 97401
www.luminarepress.com

LCCN: 2021906133
ISBN: 978-1-64388-645-9

To Olof

*Thank you for our beautiful life. Your beacon of love,
wisdom, humor, strength, and integrity shines on.
We will take it from here.*

Contents

CHAPTER ONE

What Happened?

Looking back at the year before my husband's suicide, I remember that our family had enjoyed a busy, albeit full year. Our oldest daughters, Ericka and Tatum, were away at college in California enjoying their sophomore and senior years, and we were very much relishing watching them blossom and expand their horizons. Our youngest, Emma, was a senior in high school, and we were occupied with keeping up with her activities and traipsing around the country to accompany her to college visits. My husband's surgical practice was fulfilling, as was my professor track at the university. We felt grateful.

The countdown before Olof's death seemed typical for our family rhythm. Just weeks before he died, the five of us went on our annual spring break trip, this time skiing in Whistler, Canada. We rented a house and enjoyed skiing under sunny skies, followed by après-ski dinner and family movies. There's a playful photo of him in his bright yellow ski jacket, lying on his back making snow angels with two tangerines in his eyes. He liked to be goofy. Olof and

I pinched ourselves thinking how lucky it was that two daughters' college spring breaks coincided with the other daughter's high school break. Family time. Nothing better in our book. Sure, there were the stress and angst associated with two busy careers and supporting three children's aspirations. But we were not deluded in our good fortune.

The fairy tale of being married to Olof began many years prior. Thirty-three to be exact. Olof and I began making goo-goo eyes at each other during hallway meetings in our freshman dorm. I was smitten. He was one of those enviable people who was talented at everything but didn't seem to know it. He was a straight-A, premed athlete who was musical, fun loving, and a good friend. When he broke up with his high school girlfriend fall term, I wasted no time.

We began eating all our meals together, meeting up after classes, and sharing a friend circle. We went to parties and joined an informal children's theater group and had fun putting on a production of Marlo Thomas's *Free to Be You and Me* at local libraries. We became each other's best friend, which persisted throughout college.

Olof experienced about five discrete episodes of depression over the three-decade course of our courtship and marriage, the first of which was in the spring of our freshman year. Not much was known or acknowledged about depression in those early years; thus, it did not register as a condition that warranted careful consideration or monitoring. The depression episodes always subsided. It seems strange now, but neither one of us identified as a family plagued by mental health issues.

His suicide shattered that mythical thinking.

The day before Olof died was Easter Sunday. The day began with Olof giving me my usual grand Easter basket and laying out his traditional jelly bean hunt for Emma before we dressed for church. Standard fare for Easter Sunday at the Sohlbergs. It remains disquieting to think about the day marking a holiday with resurrection from the dead as its pivotal reason for celebration. At church, Olof, Emma, and I sang the traditional hymn "Jesus Christ Is Risen Today" with gusto, as it has one of those enchanting tunes that stirs up hope and joy. You just can't help singing a little louder than is your usual practice. I remember we caught ourselves humming it throughout the day as we prepared a holiday dinner for our friends. Had some distorted aspect of a holiday lauding life after death factored into whatever darkened state Olof would descend into in the next twenty-four hours? If so, it was not evident to me. Olof blew and cleaned a dozen eggs, and we decorated them with our empty-nester friends, Reed, Tina, Paul, and Linda. Emma was the only child of the three families still at home. We talked about the fact that Olof and I would be joining our friends' empty-nester status in a mere matter of months, and our decorated eggs became elaborate testimonials to our fledgling children. Transitions. I had no idea what transition actually lay ahead.

The actual morning of Olof's death was a Monday, his day off. He took his usual bike ride and evidently got a flat tire necessitating his return home to retrieve another bike tube. He called out to me that he'd forgotten a back-up tube and yelled to have a good day. I was rushing to get to work following my morning run. I called back down the stairs to not forget to grab the errand list. I did not look up to see his face though. I had no inkling that these would be the last words that would pass between us. Try as I might, I cannot remember whether he sounded stressed or anxious or different from any other Monday as he took over the home reins for the day, and I left for the university.

After his ride, Olof had his usual Monday "Daddy lunch" with Emma. They ate together while she shared the ups and downs of her morning, and then he sat with her, per usual, while she practiced the piano for her upcoming recital. Like me, Emma did not note anything different and had no idea she would be the last person who got to enjoy her father. Credit card receipts show that the day continued with the usual Monday fare. Olof ran around town completing the errands on the list, with one extra stop. The sports store that sells handguns. This by itself was a very unusual choice for Olof. Although he grew up in Montana in a family that hunted, he was not a gun appreciator. On the contrary, I remember a heated discussion we had over the fact that he was donating more than I thought was reasonable to the Brady campaign that was working on gun control legislation. One of Olof's major political causes was reducing gun violence in our nation. An irony that plagues me daily.

I left work a half hour early that day to pick up yard signs for a school funding campaign that Olof and I had been working to support. I came home and saw that Emma's car was there, which confused me, as she was supposed to have been at a play rehearsal. I called upstairs for Olof and Emma, but the house was silent. I looked around and found packaging from an opened box on the kitchen counter that I excitedly hoped was my order from the Boden clothing catalogue. As I moved aside the packaging, I saw what appeared to be bullets—a best guess, since I had never actually laid eyes on bullets. In a split-second conclusion, my brain told me that Emma and Olof must have been taken captive by an intruder. Someone had entered our home

     McKay Moore Sohlberg

and tried to rob us, I had come home and surprised them, and now they were holding Olof and Emma upstairs. Why was that the only scenario I considered? What thief leaves a gun box on the counter? Reason and logic abandoned me. My fight-or-flight instinct led me to hysterically run to the neighbors' house to call 911. The neighbors were our good friends and told me they had heard a couple of gun shots in the last few hours but had dismissed it as firecrackers or kids. No one contemplated a different scenario.

In minutes, the SWAT team arrived, cordoned off the neighborhood, and positioned themselves accordingly, given my report that Emma and her father's cars were home, they did not answer my call, and there was foreign gun paraphernalia in the kitchen. I desperately pleaded with the officer to rush into the house to save my cherished family. But there's a protocol. They waited with their weapons poised, pointed at our house. Was this really happening? Please, God, let me wake up from this nightmare. My only allowable action was to answer a dull "no" to a dozen questions about whether there could be anyone who wished Olof harmed.

Nightmare does not even begin to express the feelings of horror and dread that I felt as I sat alone in the back seat of a police car. I thought my Beloved and my Baby Girl were gone. My world simply stopped. I think I now know what it would feel like if the earth stopped revolving on its axis. I remember that all sound ceased, and everything felt very slow. It was if I were looking through a tunnel or maybe viewing my surroundings from an underwater vantage and all activity took place on the surface. My hysteria gave way to paralysis.

After a very long time, I was told that they had located Emma, who was at school in her play rehearsal. Evidently, she had not taken her car back to school after her Monday Daddy lunch. The emotion that I felt when I received the news that she was unharmed defies words. I was in a modern day biblical story. Lazarus was raised from the dead, and she was going to be in my arms soon. Emma had returned from the World Beyond. The paralysis released me, and I climbed out of the patrol car and fell to my knees on the sidewalk, rocking my body back and forth as if getting ready to cradle Emma. When I was able, I crossed the police barrier and asked a neighbor to take me to the high school. For Emma, however, there was no relief, no joy. Minutes before, she had been a happy seventeen-year-old rehearsing for a play in which she had a lead that was due to open in two days. Now she was clinging to her mother in her high school parking lot, trying to grasp the unfathomable concept that someone may have tried to rob her house and harm her father.

Then the far more horrible truth came. We returned to the scene at our neighbors' house and were greeted by a detective who had the very hard task of telling us that they had found Olof at our home, and that he had taken his own life. He had shot himself in the head.

No way. Actually, no fucking way. Not for a moment had I entertained this as a possibility. They were wrong. Olof would not do this. He was the last person on the planet who would succumb to personal pain; besides, he hadn't been actively depressed or upset. I would know because we told each other everything. You got it wrong. Someone covered up a murder to make it look like a suicide. Emma and I yelled at them that they were wrong. It was not possible. I'm sorry, ma'am; we found a note. Well, I want to see it, insisted Emma. I don't believe it. All eyes on me. I told

     McKay Moore Sohlberg

them to show us the note. I'm sorry, ma'am; it's evidence, and we have to take it. There's a copy machine in our house. Please copy it and bring it back to my daughter and me.

There, in my neighbor's living room, sitting on her couch where I had only sat during an annual Christmas open house, I began executing what would be a never-ending list of actions to manage the aftermath of Olof's suicide. I began my first task— informing people. Someone asked if I would like help making some calls, and I remember insisting that every person would hear it from me, in my words, with my voice. But how do you call your daughters to tell them that the father with whom they had just gone skiing and talked to on the phone had shockingly ended his life and would never be there to hug, hold, and laugh with them? How do you call a mother, two brothers, and a sister to say that their cherished family of origin has been shattered by suicide? How would I call my own parents and siblings, who adored Olof and would be distraught with worry over the girls and me? If I made those phone calls, then the horrific news might actually become true, and I could not begin to fathom living a life without my soul mate, the man who had been the love of my life since I was eighteen years old. It was not a "choice" activity, however, so I channeled my courage, got out my cell phone, and pressed the "favorites" icon.

Upon learning that my beautiful Olof was gone, the sweet, privileged life I had known vanished into Eugene, Oregon's evening air. What I did not realize then was that over time, this incomprehensible nightmare would reveal many lessons. I would be forced to fashion a new life understanding. Robert Fulghum's credo *All I Really Need to Know I Learned in Kindergarten* that was displayed on a poster in my parents' home would morph into *All I Really Need to Know I Learned When My Husband Died by Suicide*. It would not be a linear process, and at times, it would be hard as hell. Although I did not know it, there would be some glimmers of light in my darkness.

The first glimmer. By some miracle, and with help from friends, Ericka and Tatum were able to fly home from Stanford to Eugene late that night. I actually don't remember who drove Emma and me to the airport, or whether I drove my own car. In an attempt to do something, however feeble, to comfort Emma, I handed her Olof's Stanford Ski Team sweatshirt that Tatum had given him—it is very thick and smelled like him. I put on my matching sweatshirt, and we departed. Emma and I numbly held each other as we waited for the sisters to come through the gate. There they were. Through some unexplainable force, they were wearing the same black-and-red club sweatshirts as Emma and me. We formed a huddle, sobbing. I remember thinking that some subconscious act of fate had dressed us alike; we were the new team. We would do this together. When we came up for air and turned around, we saw them. Our friends. The Hills, Selvens, Kratkas, Marashis, Graebners, and I don't know who else. They were lined up discretely in the background against the airport wall: Eugene, Oregon, was there. Our team was large and willing to feel their pain right along with ours. We would be joined along the way by other family, friends, and even a few strangers. We would do this together. The sight of our friends in a line on our perimeter remains one of the most powerful moments in my life. The caravan that had accompanied me on the most difficult drive of my life taught me my first new truth. It is in the dark that you can see the light.

     McKay Moore Sohlberg

I Thought Medicine Was a Science

Somebody please explain to me how a person could email the travel agent to firm up plans for a European bike trip with his wife to mark their pending empty nest, and then within hours, feel such pain that the only perceived option was to shoot himself. Hours before he died, Olof was still texting me questions about Emma's upcoming senior recital and clarifying that evening's menu. Counter to the suicide literature, he did not clean the garage, organize his affairs, or appear either more calm or more distressed; nor did he seem disengaged. He was still inserting himself in the tasks of daily life up until he ended that life. How can the neurology of a human being be wired to have such a rapid change of heart? I must have missed the signs. After the relatives left, I began to obsessively search my memory for the warning light that I'd failed to heed. I needed to understand how he got to that dark place.

I began with the recent past. I tried to recollect the conversations we had shared in the weeks preceding his death. I struggled to unearth a nuanced exchange and summon meaning to help me formulate theories and hypotheses for what led him to be suicidal. I fixated on the preceding weekend. On Saturday we had gone door to door campaigning for a local school bond. We were both active in assisting with legislative matters to support education. Olof had written a well-received letter to the editor that week encouraging the community to support this school bond. It had been pleasant walking in our assigned neighborhood, drumming up support for our cause. I followed Olof's lead in answering questions, as he was more well versed on the details of the bond. Had he seemed distracted or depressed? Was he overly intent on delivering the information? I couldn't remember any aspect of his demeanor that seemed out of the ordinary. That evening, we hung out with Emma and engaged in preparations for the Easter dinner that we were hosting the next day. We stayed up late to help the Easter Bunny hide Emma's goodies. How could I not notice something odd? He was only two days away from complete dissociation. Try as I might, however, hindsight produced nothing. The weekend offered no clues.

I progressed to looking for hints in his computer and phone. I had never had any reason to turn on his computer, but it did not take me long to guess his passwords. See? He was transparent to me. I couldn't have missed the signs about my husband whom I knew so well and loved so deeply. I even guessed correctly at security questions—his favorite place was Flathead Lake where the Sohlberg family has their cabin, and his favorite person was me. That correct guess brought a flood of new tears. I tried to remind myself that

     McKay Moore Sohlberg

he loved us fully and completely. His suicide was not about the girls and me. But what the hell caused it? I was scared that I would find some horrific piece of information that would reveal an unbearable secret. I was also scared that I would find nothing and be left in a purgatory of confusion.

I analyzed his browser searches and reviewed every email sent and received. With all due respect, his inbox might be considered boring. Work exchanges, banking communications, daily AA messages of encouragement, and family updates. Nothing out of the ordinary. The phone discovery process was equally unfruitful and extremely gut wrenching. To hear his voice message with his friendly tenor inviting his callers to leave him a message—that he would be sure to get back to them as soon as possible—made his presence palpable. He had indeed been one to respond to his callers quickly and responsibly. Olof was dependable and true to his word. Except now he would never be able to return any more calls. I kept his phone active for many months just to be able to call and hear him answer. A macabre act of irresistible self-torture. The girls showed me how to download voice messages and texts and archive them on my computer. We chronicled his last months of characteristically short, to the point, helpful messages to us. One of my last sets of texts from him had nursery photos of potential garden pots he was considering to house our columnar apple trees. Underneath the photos was the caption, "Like?" The girls had always made fun of the brevity of his texts. Little did we know that we would forever cherish every letter his precious, skilled surgeon fingers had tapped.

Friends and family also struggled to understand by analyzing their own last exchanges. His brother Rolf felt that, in retrospect, Olof's heart was not really in the training regimen that would prepare him for their pending Ironman. I then recalled a few times over the preceding two months that he had elected to sleep in instead of getting up to run with me before work at 5:30 a.m. Tina said she had thought he seemed off at our Easter dinner. Maybe. At best, our hindsights were searching guesses, full of conjecture. None of us could generate one hard potential sign strong enough to have triggered an action of concern for the man we loved deeply.

During one of my forays into investigating his computer contents, I did have a nagging memory that was triggered by looking at his automatic AA meditation emails. I remembered that we had been talking about the fact that he was no longer going to AA meetings, as he liked to cycle with a group on Saturday mornings, which conflicted with what he considered his home meeting. He was committed to his sobriety and periodically described how he was "lucky to have gotten off the elevator early" before drinking caused a problem in his life. He felt that he had the potential to misuse it. I so admired him for making that choice. I recalled that at the time of the discussion, we were driving by the church that hosted his AA meetings. I asked him if he missed going to the meetings. He responded that he didn't really have the stories to share at the AA meetings, as he had not experienced any negative repercussions from alcohol like so many people in the community whose substance abuse had robbed them of families and jobs, and that, over time, he felt less part of the group because there were not people in his same situation. He then gave a wry laugh and commented that he didn't know any alcoholics who got cured, so he should probably figure out how to fit it in his schedule again. He said something about alcoholism offering an inevitable ticket to the Next World if not attended to.

     McKay Moore Sohlberg

Was this discussion a clue? Four weeks later, I sat staring at the computer screen, wondering if perhaps he had relapsed as an unconscious ticket out of whatever mental illness hell had trapped his mind, rendering him suicidal.

I yearned to understand Olof's disease. Why hadn't we spent more time trying to figure out what had caused the five or six episodes of depression between the ages of nineteen and fifty? I obtained pharmacy records and could see that he had tapered off an antidepressant a year prior, per the recommendation of the treating psychiatrist. I had been on the conference call with the psychiatrist in Los Angeles that we were consulting. I remembered that he had told Olof to continue indefinitely on the other mood stabilizer, as that would prevent a relapse of the depression. I even found Olof's notes from the call documenting the instructions. The pharmacy records did not show the second medication being refilled. Had he obtained it somewhere else? Did he not like the side effects? Why would he not consult me?

The quest, in the aftermath of his death, to comprehend his complicated neurology in a way that I had not during his life, occupied my thoughts. I shifted my focus and started at the beginning, trying to unearth memories of the first signs of a mental health disorder. It was strange to think that, at the time when we met, we were the same age as our daughters. We were college coeds, crazy about each other. We lived on the same floor of Branner Hall, a large freshman dorm at Stanford University. We had each arrived at college with high school sweethearts back home and thus began our relationship as friends. Very soon we were fetching each other on the way to the cafeteria, riding in tandem to class, and together indulging in prototypical freshman dorm antics. I remember being attracted to his wild mop of curly, light brown hair that framed his clear blue eyes. His Swedish heritage was obvious. Olof had a strong build and was known for his speed as he attacked "the Dish" a steep run in the hills above Stanford. He exuded the Montana Western spirit and had a Boy Scout earnestness with a passion for the outdoors, but was also well read and sophisticated in his thinking and analysis, particularly for an eighteen-year-old male. He was nicknamed "Zula" by our dorm mates for his hometown, Missoula. He was friendly, well liked, and was one of the first to be sought out for beer chugging fests or for tutoring when dorm mates needed their complicated premed course content to be explained. We enjoyed the intensity of falling in love and reveled in that sweet phase where college darlings get to share all the privileges of adulthood and none of the responsibilities. What we didn't know was that by the end of the academic year, we would grow up quickly. Olof would need to take time off spring quarter due to an onset of a severe depression that seemingly came out of the blue. I called his mother to say that I thought she should come to Stanford to bring him home, as something was wrong with him.

At first he told me he thought he had a weird virus. He described it as a tight sensation of pain in his chest or around his heart. Then he tried to figure out what was making him feel sad. Perhaps it was the pressures of a competitive premed track? He had a 4.0 GPA that was earned without much angst, so that theory didn't feel quite right. Over the course of weeks, he began having trouble getting up and going to class and required me to stand at his bedside and coax him out of his dorm room. At the time, unlike today, depression and mental illness were not common concepts familiar to college kids. I remember being baffled by his symptoms and then being scared. After I called his mom, his parents took him home to Missoula, where they promptly took him to a psychiatrist.

Olof and I stayed in touch through letters and landline phone calls, as there were no cell phones in that era. He was put on some medications—it was before the days of the selective serotonin reuptake inhibitor (SSRI) antidepressants used so widely today, and he said they treated him with an amphetamine that was an experimental practice for severe depression. His father, Steve, an obstetrician/gynecologist and part of the local medical community, had his colleague treat Olof. Steve died before Olof's suicide, a chronology for which I've often been grateful, as he would have been devastated by Olof's passing. However, I would love to have had his physician's perspective to help me better understand that period during our freshman year when Olof came home. The treatment, the initial diagnosis, and Steve's insights might help me connect some medical dots.

After initial treatment, Olof began working for a family friend who had a roofing business and got ready to return to Stanford for summer school. He was better. And then he got *too* better. He had a full blown manic episode, replete with delusions of grandeur, inability to sleep, racing thoughts, and erratic behavior. It was the only manic episode that he ever experienced, and many years later we were told by a psychiatrist that the prescribed amphetamines likely kicked off the manic phase and were no longer a treatment used today. Indeed, it is now known that the most commonly prescribed class of antidepressants, SSRIs, can actually worsen symptoms in people who have bipolar disorder.

Of course, I learned these facts after my Olof was gone. Why didn't his internist and local psychiatrist know this?

While I feel anger at the medical community that Olof bravely consulted on the few occasions when he was symptomatic, I hold no such anger toward the initial providers, as there was so much less known. I remember after the trial with the amphetamines thirty years prior that Olof's dad told me, "I think he has manic depression," which was the term used for bipolar disorder at the time. In spite of their concern, his parents left for a long-planned European tour, and Olof departed for California to visit me at my parents' house on his way to Stanford to attend summer school. Unbeknownst to me and my family, he was manic.

Ironically, the weird thing was that he just didn't seem that weird. He had endless energy and did things that made me laugh, like saying we should run everywhere instead of walking so we would become really fit. Yes, we actually ran from the car into the grocery store. He even hopped a few parking lot benches along the way. He organized my parents' refrigerator, creating an impressive artistic structure out of deli meat and condiment jars. My family thought it was funny and imaginative. He woke up my sports-enthused younger brother at the crack of dawn and dragged him to a nearby lake and conned people into taking them waterskiing. Olof told random boaters that he was a professional waterskier, and given Olof actually could ski barefoot, backward, and do a whole host of tricks, they believed him. He gave my brother a lake day adventure that he talked about for years. Olof also began a campaign to raise money for some cause whose name I can no longer remember. I do, however, remember thinking he was expansive and made things happen. What I now know were delusions of grandeur common to mania, seemed then like actions of being intentional and living

    McKay Moore Sohlberg

fully. While he had the heightened energy, euphoria, and creativity common to a manic state, he did not exhibit the irritability and defensiveness, reckless spending, or inappropriate sexual activity that is also common to this condition. He had been brilliant prior to becoming ill, so it was easy to believe that he was simply energetic and ecstatic, happy to no longer be depressed. An erroneous conclusion. Although I did not realize it, he was very sick.

By the beginning of fall term of our sophomore year, Olof had calmed down. We both enrolled in a seminar class titled Psychopathology that satisfied one of our human biology major requirements. As we sat together in lecture and learned about unipolar and bipolar depression, we looked at each other wide-eyed, and I whispered, "Maybe that's what you had." It seems inconceivable to me now that we didn't go running to seek medical guidance or call up his parents or mull it over more. But he was "normal" again, and we thought of the depression as past tense. Cured. I also need to remind myself that we were young, not yet twenty, and the state of knowledge at that time was limited and the medication options few. I'm guessing that Olof did not like to think about the disease unless forced to, as everything I've read about the depressed state suggests that it is nothing short of torture. I'm guessing, because I never asked.

Olof had one more bout of depression during college. He sought help at the student health center and was put on medication. I don't remember what class of drugs he was on, just that it made him extremely groggy. In spite of missing more than a few classes and needing me and our friend Brian to drag him out of bed, Olof maintained a perfect GPA, and eventually weaned himself off the medication. We were back in business. We enjoyed a close circle of college friends, studied hard, played on intramural teams, went to parties and dances, and took each other on romantic dates. Other than the two pronounced periods of depression during our undergraduate years, we enjoyed a quintessential college life. I remember feeling quite proud watching his Phi Beta Kappa ceremony where he was rewarded for excelling in his biochemistry concentration while deeply pursuing coursework in the humanities. My parents and his parents were in attendance. We laughed about the boring speaker, and I don't think any of us worried about a long-term mental health disorder. It was hard to be concerned. Olof and I began excitedly talking about marriage and made a private, giddy decision to announce our engagement during the first Christmas after college. I was going to marry the smartest, kindest, cutest, strongest, funniest person on the planet. And I did. I also married someone who had mental illness.

Olof experienced another depressive episode between medical school and residency. It was much more mild, and again, Olof sought help, took the drugs until he could no longer stand the side effects, and then weaned himself with physician support. I remember that it was hard to see him despondent, and I naively felt that if I said the right optimistic statement, I might make him feel better. Ultimately, however, the cycle was short and the drugs helped, and the worry receded. With years between episodes, it was easy to dismiss concerns. As I write the course of his illness for the very first time, I am struck by what clearly was a pattern, but one that we either repressed or was too subtle or lost in the busyness of life for us to attend to. Other than the one manic episode after the experimental drug treatment in Missoula, his illness was characterized

     McKay Moore Sohlberg

by depression without mania or swings. It would be almost eighteen years until a doctor would tell him that he likely had some background "cycling" with high and low mood alterations that he just powered through or did not recognize as being abnormal.

Eighteen years, age thirty to forty-eight, is a very long hiatus to be symptom free. Long enough that an illness is all but forgotten, at least for the adoring spouse. Long enough to bring three beautiful daughters into the world, launch two full, rewarding careers, establish a community of remarkable friends in our small university town, explore the great outdoors together, spend time with our wonderful extended family, and live fully. Now this period plagues me, however. Was he really okay? Did he suffer silently? I remember that our smug pillow talk was of the ilk, "We did it. We made the life we desired." Did he just try to please me? It is common for mental illness to emerge in late adolescence. I cling to the hope that the chemical processes responsible for that onset calmed down after he got through his twenties. My choice narrative is that his neurology cooperated for the critical years of raising our girls and forming deep family connections. I glean comfort from the research that suggests the settling of structural and developmental brain changes that is associated with the end of adolescence could account for a sustained healthy state.

Olof's next notable mental health juncture was his decision that he was not a healthy drinker. He was forty-seven. I was working on my computer one evening answering student emails, and he came to me and said he believed he was an alcoholic. He confessed that during the preceding three months there had been evenings when I was working that he would stealthily make himself a drink, and that the occasions were increasing. It had not occurred during the day, but on some evenings and weekends, and he had quietly purchased liquor to support the increasing habit. We had experienced several arguments, silly conflicts whose topics I can't even remember, and it made sense that, in retrospect, he had been drinking. He was scared and very ashamed. I so badly want to write that I embraced him and gave him unconditional support, but I would be lying. The truth is that initially I was angry that he had deceived me and focused on that, rather than his courage to face his disease. I so want a do-over.

The next day he went to talk to some people at a local drug and alcohol treatment facility who told him that he did not need intervention but would benefit from AA. For three years, that was a source of support and community that he fully embraced. He wrote an email to his family and told our friends and daughters about his vulnerability to alcohol, participation in AA, and decision to be sober. Family and friends were surprised since alcohol had not been a problem that they had noted. We did some couples counseling that helped me let go of my hurt feelings and become a better support. Words cannot express how proud I am of Olof's decision and actions around realizing his vulnerability. There was no catalyst other than his own conscience and desire to be his best self. He was brave, honest, and committed. At the time, I thought he might have begun self-medicating with alcohol to manage stress around work as his group had built a surgery center and expanded their practice. Now, I suspect the self-medicating was because he was subconsciously experiencing some mood disruptions and the depression cycling that would begin to plague him once again in one year's time. Middle age would bring a recurrence of the depression.

 McKay Moore Sohlberg

Retrospection has led me to suspect his bipolar disorder was, at least in part, due to hormonal fluctuations. In the same way that the depression had a sudden onset in the period of late adolescence, this next bout coincided with a diagnosis of an endocrine disorder that changed his hormonal status. Around the time Olof stopped drinking, he saw a specialist and was put on full replacement of thyroid hormone and testosterone. A brain scan showed a condition called *empty sella syndrome* causing a reduction in the pituitary gland, which could explain his endocrine failures. As the hormones were all synthetically replaceable, it seemed like a curable problem. True to character, Olof did not whine about having a medical condition and assured me that this was not a big deal. No muss no fuss. He added two new prescriptions to his daily regimen, celebrated the abatement of his symptoms, and the good life continued.

And then it happened. A year later, the depression returned. But this time it was intractable.

He called his internist and said he was experiencing significant depression. The internist offered to prescribe antidepressants over the phone, but Olof said he wanted a face-to-face appointment. I went with him. We asked about the possible relationship of the depression recurrence to his endocrine problem. We reviewed Olof's mental health history in detail, including his attendance at AA. I fretted and was angsty with the doctor and pressed him for a magic bullet or a systematic plan to improve Olof's state. We left with a prescription for the preferred antidepressant of the day. That's it. We were offered no further mental health information or signs to watch for, no exploration of possible bipolar disease, no referrals, and most importantly, no suicide evaluation. This would happen two more times with different doctors. Why did they not investigate further? I suspect that they just did not think Olof could be that ill. He was a very well-respected surgeon and family man with a robust practice and high level of community engagement. He had self-referred and talked openly about his symptoms. I'm guessing these qualities kept him off the worry radar of the treating physicians. It seemed that they believed he had a garden variety depression that could be effectively managed with medication.

But it was not effectively managed. Olof told me he was scared and that every day he was struggling to initiate and do what he wanted to do. Finally we did some research—and with the help of our oldest physician friend, Brian, who had gone to Stanford with us—we obtained an appointment with a world expert in psychopharmacology who specialized in depression for "high functioning" patients (aka professionals with money who would fly to Los Angeles). Ironically, this psychiatrist was president of the American Foundation for Suicide Prevention. He was a chemical wizard and figured out a cocktail that matched Olof's symptoms that included a stimulant and mood stabilizer. It did the trick. Within months, we were back in business. Until we weren't. Two years later, my beloved Olof would die by suicide.

The Los Angeles psychiatrist followed Olof by phone and weaned him off one of the medications and firmly told him that he would need to stay on the other one for life. Here's where my fact trail runs dry, and I am left with a handful of guesses and assumptions. I do not know whether Olof stayed on the medication as directed by the psychiatrist. Whatever, the case, I assume that his depression started to reoccur, and this time it would've been only

     McKay Moore Sohlberg

months, not years, after having been treated. I assume that his disease had more dark, dissociative features than before, and that as Olof was aging, the disease was changing. I assume that Olof grit his way through the intermittent dark, determined to not let it disrupt the family. Grit is a Sohlberg modus operandi. My guess is that he knew that the cycles were getting closer, and that he was scared there would be no more options. Maybe there was so much to do with work and an active family life that he didn't have a chance to be really sick. Maybe the disease creates the dark thoughts and there is no rational interpretation. What I do know, without a doubt, is that he continued being a very fine physician, community member, friend, and most importantly to him, husband and father, until the end. Olof was the one suffering during that time, and if I am honest with this history lesson, despite the torment it causes me, the truth is he suffered alone in this last bout of depression.

Suicide leaves families spinning in their own quest to figure out what happened. It also leaves them vulnerable to everyone else's suppositions and theories. There was the "physician pressure theory" given the statistics on the high numbers of physicians with Olof's profile who die by suicide. I heard lots about Olof's busy practice. Then there was the "shame from alcohol relapse theory," which assumed he had relapsed and could not handle the disgrace. This theory tended to be emphasized by those in that club. The notion that could invoke a private fury was the "buried secret theory." It was a pretty good secret, since the gambling, girlfriend, or financial ruin has yet to surface. There was also the history reconstruction where his highly productive nature was recast as evidence for a lifetime of mania. I learned not to protest too loudly to people's theories and interpretations. Like me, they were grieving and just trying to make rational sense of the irrational. I would spit out my retorts silently: "You might want to look up the definition of *manic*. Manic people don't come home from work in the evening, cook a family dinner, help with homework, and then read quietly before bed." I'd silently think my defense and then nod, "maybe…" I suppose on one level, however, I appreciated it when people told me what they were thinking and engaged in a topic that was always on my mind. This was a much preferred option over the uncomfortable shift and breaking of eye contact if his name came up, a necessary strategy to avoid the possibility that we might acknowledge the "s" word.

My own theory is that of a Perfect Storm. A Disease-Trifecta. His genetic makeup gave him bipolar disorder, alcohol vulnerability, and hormonal instability. It also made him an extraordinary human being.

One of the most cogent writings on suicide, perhaps the only one that I felt captured my own hunches and circumstances, was the escapism theory written about by Roy Baumeister in 1990, who frames suicide as an escape from psychological pain that is usually due to an acute state of mind. The theory suggests that those who are suicidal are not always aware of it, and there are certain thought conditions that must be in place for it to occur. The suicidal mind cannot be understood by imposing our rational theories, as there is a certain level of dissociation that has to be in place. Not every person who is depressed attempts suicide and not every person who dies by suicide is depressed. The conditions that have to be in place for a suicidal mind include some factors that at first glance seem paradoxical but resonated with my take on Olof. For example, having an

     McKay Moore Sohlberg

ideal life can sometimes heighten the risk if you have other factors because there is such a discrepancy between what you have known and what your disease makes you feel. High achievers may be more at risk. I think I read the literature because it let me stay in my head and avoid my heart. It also gave me the illusion of understanding that I craved.

In my quest to understand Olof's suicide in the initial years after his death, I felt tethered to a mental treadmill where I engaged in repetitive list making. It was as if the ultimate explanation would reveal itself if I just kept sorting and reanalyzing the data. I cannot explain why this seemed like a necessary path to feeling better. One list that I constantly fashioned contained what, to me, were the essential indisputable facts—those things that I knew, without a doubt, to be true. This list included beliefs like Olof's deep love for me and the girls and my knowledge that he was born with some type of brain chemical imbalance. I also mentally composed lists of things that seemed likely or probable. My supposition about the changing nature of his disease during middle age and a probable alcohol relapse as a response to the recurrence of depression are sample occupants on this list. The third list housed my mystery items—those scary things that I would never know and had no basis for even guessing, but that plagued me at my core. Did he discontinue his medication? How long had he been aware of his suicidal thoughts? What happened that afternoon to induce such a drastic and fatal change in behavior? I hated this list. Still, knowing all that I knew and didn't know, and acknowledging the inevitable brutal end, there was one thing I knew for sure that was at the top of list number one. I would do it all again.

A little over three years after Olof died, I received a letter in the mail that at least temporarily quieted my questions and search for explanations. The letter had been forwarded from Olof's medical office. In the envelope was a birth announcement for a baby whose name I did not recognize. The envelope also contained a handwritten letter beginning *Dear Mrs. Sohlberg, In June 2009, our five-year-old daughter, our only child, was killed by a drunk driver...*The letter chronicled the couple's devastation and desperate wish to have a vasectomy reversal by a urologist so that they might have a chance to have another child. They did not have medical insurance and could not afford the procedure. The letter shared how Olof had quietly told them not to worry and performed the procedure in his surgery center. They assumed that he had somehow managed to get all the medical fees waived, as the couple was never billed. They wrote that it had taken several years, but the procedure had been successful. The looping handwriting detailed the indescribable joy of the birth of their infant son that fall, three years after Olof's death. They ended the letter by asking if I would *please accept their gratitude on Dr. Sohlberg's behalf.* They did not express condolences or hint at the tragedy of Olof's death. They did not even mention it. It was clear the couple was not concerned with how or why he died. What he accomplished while he was alive was all that mattered to these people. I read the letter over and over and felt the urgency to understand the conditions explaining his death fade. An astounding set of circumstances had rendered the search for rational explanations irrelevant. Olof's death did not erase his life. Quite the contrary, he continued to give life even after he was gone.

 McKay Moore Sohlberg

Now What?

Now what? In the early months after Olof's death, I would sit at the kitchen table, stare out the window, and watch the comings and goings at the bird feeder. The chickadees and nuthatches flitted about anxiously as if afflicted with some type of avian attention deficit disorder, seemingly unable to commit to eating their seed or to hanging out on the perch for more than a few nanoseconds. I related. I could not find a rhythm or purpose, and struggled to figure out how to settle enough to do the next right thing.

I remember enumerating my life roles in a desperate attempt to find solace that I still had a place and belonged in the schema of those left living. Olof and I had been together since our teens, and I'd never loved another man. We had enjoyed a wonderful interdependence that required both parties in order for each of us to function. Without him, was I still a professor? Check. That seemed like an honest role I could still claim. I sat at my computer in the same office, on the same campus where I had been employed for seventeen years. Graduate students, colleagues, and patients with brain injuries all showed up with expectations that I would do the activities that I was trained to carry out, and mostly, I think I delivered. Was I still a mother? Major check, but it was altered. Motherhood became my reason, but I now needed to expand it to include some fatherhood. The girls' welfare consumed my every moment. I was glued to my cell phone. Sometimes during important meetings or teaching, I mustered the courage to switch it to the vibration mode, but it was never off. If the children called, I excused myself and took the call. I was on call 24-7 to help them through whatever arose, whenever they needed it. What about the role of friendship—could I still consider myself a loyal and good friend? Iffy. I was blessed with close, deep friendships, and prior to Olof's death, I would have described myself as a present, caring friend who was also fun. Now the friendships were lopsided. I was wounded, so I took. And the friends gave. Coffee chats, running talks, shared glasses of wine, all of these get-togethers were dominated by my tears and a need to reminisce and talk aloud about what my girls might need. It was all I had to give to the conversation. Still a woman? Iffy again. I thought I was a feminist, but quickly learned—maybe not so much. I did not feel like a woman without my man. I put up some good fronts, but being solo at the dinner invites was always followed by crying myself to sleep once I was home and had privacy to do so.

A New Self

Thus began a slow and painful redefinition of myself that forced me to reclaim some roles in new and different ways and let go of others. The difficulty of Olof's death was compounded by the fact that it coincided with me beginning the empty nest phase. I wished the identity reconstruction

 McKay Moore Sohlberg

could have been done surgically rather than experientially. It would've been quicker, and I could have slept through it.

My friends and colleagues at my university created a sanctuary of normal and gave me perhaps the one role that wasn't completely altered by Olof's death and the girls' leavings. Out of my sight, the faculty and staff worked extra to take up the slack by my absence and my limited productivity. When I was there, they consulted me and helped me rejoin the faculty. If my office door was shut, they gave me space and pretended not to notice the puffy eyes.

I had to quickly return to work, as I was in the midst of evaluating over twenty masters' projects where the students were scheduled to present their capstone projects in three weeks. Within two weeks of Olof's death, I was reviewing and grading student papers. Editing papers created an interesting backdrop to my early grief. Grief has its own evolving syntax. Early on, there are only short clauses and single words. The punctuation consists largely of question marks and ellipses denoting unfinished thoughts and events. The grammar then becomes more complex with contrastive clauses linked by conjunctions such as *although, albeit, but*. With time, the punctuation becomes more varied, although not conventional. Periods, exclamation points, and dashes start to dot the page. Syntactical rules are largely ignored, and run-on sentences are the new norm. As I marked up the students' papers and struggled to formulate helpful feedback, I realized that the literal and symbolic had joined. My metaphorical syntax was distorted along with my actual ability to generate coherent paragraphs. Since that time, my writing fluency has continued to be a litmus test for my state of adjustment.

My role in the homemaking realm was even less intact. Grocery shopping initially loomed large as a very scary activity that was hard to reclaim. I had been able to evade it because the food drop-offs from a caring community were quite prolific. Eventually, however, I needed to go to the store for a few items. My saint sister, Erika (Beester to me), had abandoned her family and work to travel from her home in Paris to stay with me as I got my feet on the ground. She was the one who babysat me on my very first trip to the market. I remember that outing as surreal. I had no idea how loaded grocery shopping could be. People's grocery carts tell you a lot. Admit it. You've looked at some person who is carrying more than a few extra pounds and thought, "Honey, let me help you—lose the Fritos and Häagen-Dazs and go get some veggies." Never again will I judge. I looked down at my cart with a tremendous sense of humility. I told my sister that I guess I only needed a few apples and put the others back. How long would it take one person to get through a quart of yogurt? It suddenly looked rather large—would it spoil? Maybe I should get a couple of smaller containers? My grocery cart was no longer a family cart. It was not even an empty-nester, couples cart. Basically, the cart screamed *this shopper lives ALONE!* In my narcissistic grief state, I imagined that everyone in the store was looking at my cart and inwardly shaking their heads about the pathetic plight of this poor, single, fellow shopper.

I did have one place, however, where I felt comfortable. The car. I liked being in the car. This is somewhat ironic as I was not the driver in the family. When we were together, Olof drove. Long car trips? Olof drove every mile. He liked to drive, and I did not. I was in charge of road snacks, car games, and managing the books on tape. He was responsible for all tasks related to navigation. Another nice marital arrangement. I was now a solo driver, however,

   McKay Moore Sohlberg

and surprisingly it was one of the few early places where I found solace. Maybe it was because I felt normal when I was driving. The guy next to you at the traffic signal does not look over and give the knowing glance, "Ah yes, your husband just died. And I believe it was by suicide." No, he honks at you if you start to veer into his lane because you are distracted, treating you like every other driver on the road. I could pretend in the car. Maybe I also liked being in the car because it was a cocoon of sorts. It was a small controlled space that surrounded me—a modern womb for grown-ups. It was one of the few places where I talked to Olof aloud. A lot of my early statements were about reassurance. I had this nagging fear that somehow he was in a suspended, tortured state of afterlife, full of self-loathing for having given into his pain and abandoned us. I'd try to soothe him: "I'm going to figure things out. You rest." I think I entertained a fantasy that I would eventually be able to drive home to him.

Being the family driver was one of many new roles that I claimed by default. One of the most important drives I took was the road trip with the three girls as we moved Ericka's belongings home after her college graduation. At Ericka's encouragement, we had celebrated her Stanford graduation exactly as planned, just weeks after Olof's death. We held the party that Olof and I had begun organizing. My wonderful in-laws made the trek from Oregon and Montana to mark Ericka's accomplishment along with Olof's best college friend, Brian. I had flown in late in the event schedule as Emma was graduating from high school in Eugene with a parallel set of celebrations. My parents attended the parent events to fill in the gaps until I got there. My village was ensuring that our lives moved forward. I had a sense of doing the pomp and circumstance in part to honor Olof, whose amazing parenting had contributed to the girls reaching their goals. Then the parties were over. The Phi Beta Kappa and graduation diplomas had been delivered, and Olof's truck was packed with four years of college belongings.

Sister-in-law Kristen worked the Sohlberg magic; they can pack more items into the volume of available car space than is allowable by the laws of physics. She did it just like her brother would have. I swear there must be a packing gene. The girls and I started home for Eugene. As I headed north on Interstate 5, my metaphorical and literal worlds collided once again. Literally and symbolically, I was the driver on the trip. The girls were fast asleep, worn out from the emotion of the festivities and from trying to adjust to their new circumstance. It was my job to safely steer us forward.

Some roles disappear instantly with the death of a spouse. Those are the roles that you hold by proxy because of your partner. For me, a very bitter pill was my initial perceived separation from the medical community. Being a medical family means that the identity of every single person in the family is at least in part medical. Ours was particularly pronounced because Olof was one of the fortunate few whose job was a calling. He loved being a urologist. I received hundreds of letters from patients who clearly felt Olof's commitment to them. Being a surgeon was part of his very fabric, and by association, I felt it too. Longevity contributed to my sense of ownership. I had been part of the medical journey for a long time. Four years of college premed studies, four years of medical school, six years of residency, the joining of a small private practice, the merging of several practices, the building of a surgery center:

 McKay Moore Sohlberg

these were major personal life phases for me, as well as for Olof. I admit that after all those years, I felt like a pseudo doctor. Seriously, I know a lot about prostate cancer treatment options, and if you ask me some basic bread-and-butter urology questions, I think you would be impressed. But then it was over. Really over. The medical community was surprisingly quiet, especially compared to the outpouring from people in contexts we knew much less well. Healers are complicated and just as human as the rest of us.

My commitment to telling the light and the dark means sharing the disappointments. I received neither call nor note from the psychiatrist in town who had last treated Olof. Bitterness makes you do weird things. I went so far as to look up the practice guidelines governing psychiatrists and learned that they do allow for contacting the surviving family of a patient who dies by suicide. *So the doctor could have called me.* Several of Olof's closest medical partners, people he had actively supported and who were friends, did not visit to express condolences or offer help. I had asked for some help in cleaning out his office, but none of these partners who I considered his close friends and colleagues were available. I had to actively work to relinquish bitterness and remember that they had to deal with their own loss and emotional complexities around his suicide. It was his staff who emailed me to check in and share the goings on and invited me to gatherings. I missed Olof's work stories. I missed being part of our town's medical world. As I nursed a sense of abandonment, the exceptions to the silence came.

One night I found myself making a solo trip to the emergency room when I woke up with pain that scared me. I was the only parent the girls had left, and my worst-case scenario brain was in overdrive. The girls had no more spare tires for parents. I walked into the emergency room through a different door than usual. When you are a doctor's spouse, you hold privileges, like not waiting in the waiting room and going straight back to see the person who is on call that night. If you have a medical question or need, your friends and colleagues are there to help you. You do not experience the usual barriers to healthcare access. I registered myself and sat next to who I believe were two people who were homeless and had experienced some type of altercation with resulting wounds that were poorly bandaged with dirty rags. They smelled and sounded like they had taken advantage of the anesthetic found in a wine bottle. I waited my turn. They were first. I started sensing the prickly, bitter feeling of privilege—after all, hadn't I earned a place first in line with all my years in the medical community? But like the Grinch, as I looked over at my waiting room comrades with lacerations on their faces and hands, my heart grew three sizes. Why should I go before them? They were down on their luck, and I was down on mine. They had life stories, and so did I. I was part of humanity. It's hard to describe, but I felt a glorious sense of belonging. I was a regular person. We were all regular people. I also was anticipating that I would know the ER doctor, and my patience and grace would be duly rewarded.

Not so. After I was finally ushered to my cubicle, Dr. Hayes came in and introduced himself. Zero recognition. I gave my name, thinking he'd say, "Oh—Sohlberg, I'm so very sorry. I knew your husband; he was wonderful." No such luck. He ran some tests but had to leave to care for more urgent patients. There, in the wee hours before dawn, I got a lesson in being a regular person—I

     McKay Moore Sohlberg

felt vulnerable and anonymous, but at least part of a caring system. Things were going to be okay. As I lay there receiving IV antibiotics, Dr. Hayes returned. The emergency room had cleared out, and he had some time to chat. It was then that he told me he had known Olof, and that he had worked with Olof in the ER several days before he died. He told me that Olof was known not just for being a skilled surgeon but for being a devoted family man. This doctor knew the ages and schools of my girls. Dr. Hayes's gifts that night were many and important. He gave me a chance to experience being a regular person on my own and a part of everyday humanity. Paradoxically, I felt sufficient as an individual while being part of the grand scheme called Life. He showed me that I was still part of the medical community, but that it wasn't important for the reasons I was missing. He gave me a precious gift of knowing about Olof's last days at work. And he gave me antibiotics.

There have been others who helped me feel connected to the medical arena that I sorely missed. Reed and Tina, our very dear friends, both of whom are physicians and shared major medical practice karma with Olof, were open and raw about their own pain of losing him, not only as a close friend, but as their colleague. They, along with others, fed me excerpts of conversations with patients they had in common with Olof, and reminded me what a talented and respected physician he had been. My own physician, Melissa Edwards, shared some of the triumphs from a medical committee in which Olof had served an instrumental role, and credited his early vision. It helped to hear how much he was missed. Suicide creates disquiet when survivors fear that their loved one's mechanism of death will negatively supplant all the good in that person's life. Connie and Dave DiMarco, partners in Olof's group, reached out not because they felt sorry for me, but because they admired Olof and felt inspired by our family. Connie would text me from the hospital: "I just came out of surgery and found myself looking for Olof to consult with. I miss him." Dave started texting me his bike racing times. Olof had mentored him in this sport, and he had a previous habit of texting his times to Olof. Another newer partner, Chris Kyle, reached out to my daughter Ericka as she began considering going into urology and encouraged her. Later, our friend Kiya, a neurosurgeon in town, would become president of his association and honor Olof and lead his specialty in physician wellness. While I wished the medical community had reached out more globally to the girls and me, there were individuals who helped me transition from current to former medical spouse by celebrating and cementing the past. They honored Olof, and in so doing, helped us heal.

Grief has an uncomfortable way of rendering a person a bit narcissistic. This is hard to admit, but I'm not sure there is any way around it. It's one of those untalked about grief issues. Everyone encourages you to "focus on your own needs," "avoid *should*," "take a buy whenever you don't want to do something." I did not really need this counsel, however, because I was simply unable to focus on issues outside my own sphere. My brain and heart were simply too occupied with fear, sadness, and the demands of figuring out basic life tasks like paying the mortgage. Hence, one of the roles that has been slowest to recover is that of citizen. I like to think of myself as an engaged citizen who is attentive to the events in my community,

    McKay Moore Sohlberg

nation, and the world. When Olof died, my community engagement was reduced to the community of my three children. That was all that mattered. Each evening, I recycled the paper unread. I had no idea of the news events that occurred in our world for many months after Olof died. I remember joking to Cary and Jani on one of our morning runs, "Is Obama still president?" Truth be told, it was only a partial joke.

The same goes for reading. I had been a voracious reader. Now books felt aversive. I worried there was something wrong with me, as the grief books didn't mention this symptom. I read for work but could not get beyond page one of a novel. It was like I had no patience for someone else's story. Movies and TV were even harder to relate to. It bothered me greatly, and I worried that my stress had led to cognitive changes. Was it an attention or information processing deficit? Was it an inability to shift from thinking about my own story to someone's fictional account? Regardless, it was just one more example that I was no longer my same me. The first whole book I read was Tina Fey's *Bossypants*. It was a Christmas present from my brother—not fiction, a real woman's memoir with dry humor and sarcasm, a perfect bridge back to literacy. I graduated to stories about female refugees and relished *Little Bee* and *The Bite of the Mango*. I think I liked the inspiration of reading about lives completely shattered amidst the resilience to start again. Misery loves company, but she needs hope.

So Much to Learn and Do

There was so much I had to learn. My identity reconstruction was in part driven by a list of essential tasks that I needed to master if I did not want to lose my house or get into hot water with the IRS. This part of my story is embarrassing. It is with no small amount of shame that I had to come to terms with fundamental gaps in basic knowledge. I was like Rip Van Winkle waking up to the modern era at age fifty-one. Electronic bill pay, car insurance, and Comcast were complete mysteries. The completion of vital life tasks was further complicated by the fact that everything required a password—none of which I knew. I had daily phone meltdowns when trying to talk to service people who needed passwords or information that I did not possess. I made a call to inquire about how to pay my gas bill and explained to the service agent that my husband had passed away. I was told that since the sole customer on the account was no longer at the documented residence, they would need to turn off the gas immediately. Explaining that I had lived at the residence for twenty years and shared the name of the absent customer and even birthed his children was not compelling. There are company policies, you know. They actually sent me a welcome packet for new customers. Olof clearly had not planned his death, as there was no road map for handling the bazillion responsibilities in the realm of finances and home management that he executed with seeming ease. The learning curve was steep and scary.

In the spirit of true confession—I was starting at ground zero, actually subzero in a few departments. I had never looked at an EOB (*explanation of benefits*, for any other adults starting at ground zero) and asked my friends why medical insurance would send a piece of paper telling you what you were *going* to owe instead of just sending you a bill? Seems kind of mean to give you the bad news twice.

  McKay Moore Sohlberg

My confusion was ignited at a bank meeting when they kept referring to a CD. Why would they be referencing music? Why was the insurance agent concerned about my umbrella policy? Something to do with living in rainy Oregon, so you need extra insurance coverage? Early on, I received a check refund for something Olof had ordered—do people still write "for deposit only" on checks? The last paper check I had deposited was thirty years prior when I was in college. Ground subzero. Going to the mailbox inevitably evoked a treasure hunt for some elusive piece of knowledge about how to read, let alone respond to, a bill. Every system is different and transparency is clearly not the goal. I had been in charge of opening and responding to personal correspondence. How did he do all the rest?

In my defense, Olof and I had grown up together and had perfected the Division of Labor that good marriages in busy families learn how to fully leverage. We had committees, subcommittees, domain manager, and project manager roles quite evolved and functional. It's just that the tasks he was in charge of seemed so critical and enigmatic. My already fractured sense of self became more vulnerable as I realized that I was missing knowledge of some basic tasks of daily living. I started operating by two essential principles:

Plug the biggest holes in the dike first. I have a medical background and understand triage. Figure out how to pay bills and insurance first. Then worry about the running toilet and mold in the shower.

Call on your family, friends, and acquaintances with knowledge in the areas you lack, and ask questions. If you don't know anyone, ask a stranger. Write down the answers or you will forget.

I have experience managing interdisciplinary research projects and running a university training program, yet I felt totally flummoxed on a daily basis. I needed rudimentary knowledge before my organizational skills would be remotely useful. I asked a lot of embarrassingly basic questions and am happy to share that not once in three years did I ever experience a hint of ridicule or "you've got to be kidding me—are you really asking this question?" from a family member, friend, banker, accountant, attorney, or credit card agent. It is true. People want to help, or at least they make you feel like they do. I am, by nature, a problem solver, one of those rational types who prides herself on accomplishing tasks with efficiency and ingenuity. While I was frustrated and overwhelmed that my usual tactics were not sufficient, I mobilized my internal drive and tried to address the myriad roadblocks I encountered each day.

Task mastery has been steady, and my organizational chart is getting filled out. Full disclosure in my chart below reveals that there are still some basics to go, but now instead of crying when I realize I do not yet know how to do something, I whistle Helen Reddy's "I Am Woman," and usually I figure it out (or delegate—an essential principle that I had well honed long before widowhood).

    McKay Moore Sohlberg

DIVISION OF LABOR
My Organizational Chart

	Primary Manager		
LIFE DOMAIN			
Domain Manager	*(Before)*	*(In Year One)*	*(In Year Three)*
Domain subtasks	*(Before)*	*(In Year One)*	*(In Year Three)*

EN Empty Nest—task no longer relevant | **--** Abandoned task | **Helper** Paid support

FINANCES	**(Before)**	**(Year One)**	**(Year Three)**
Domain Manager	***Olof***	***Me***	***Me***
Primary wage earner	Olof	Me	Me
Secondary wage earner	Me	--	--
Monthly bills	Olof	Me & Friends	Me
Tax info to accountant	Olof	My Dad	Me
Retirement plan	Olof	Helper	Me & Helper

FOOD MANAGEMENT	**(Before)**	**(Year One)**	**(Year Three)**
Domain Manager	***Me***	***Me***	***Me***
Menu planning	Me	Me & Friends	Me
Grocery shopping	Olof & Me	Me	Me
Packing weekly lunches	Me	Me	Me
Weekday dinners	Me	Me & Friends	Me
Weekend meals	Olof	Me & Friends	Me

Parties/gatherings	Me & Olof	Me & Friends	Me
BBQ	Olof	Friends	Me

EDUCATION	(Before)	(Year One)	(Year Three)
Domain Manager	**Me**	**Me**	**Me**
Tracking classes/programs	Me	EN	EN
School communication	Me	EN	EN
Math/science support	Olof	EN	EN
Paper edits	Me	Me	Me
Volunteer (PTA, classes)	Olof & Me	EN	EN
Applications—college/ medical school	Me	Me	Me
Career/school advising	Olof & Me	Me	Me

HOUSE MANAGEMENT	(Before)	(Year One)	(Year Three)
Domain Manager	**Olof**	**Me & Helper**	**Me**
Weekly cleaning	Helper	Helper	Helper
Laundry	Me	Me	Me
Routine maintenance	Olof & Me	Friends	Me & Friends
Call plumber, electrician, etc.	Olof	Me	Me
Remodeling & updating	Olof	--	--
Decorating	Me	--	Me
Pest control—mice, dead birds	Olof	Friends	Friends
Pest control—spiders, bees	Me	Me	Me

GARDEN MANAGEMENT	(Before)	(Year One)	(Year Three)
Domain Manager	*Me*	*Me*	*Me*
Plant selection	Me	--	Me
Digging holes/ heavy labor	Olof & Helper	Helper	Helper
Weekend gardening chores	Olof & Me	Helper	Me & Helper
Irrigation	Olof	Helper	Helper
Home garden picnics	Me	--	Me

TRAVEL & RECREATION	(Before)	(Year One)	(Year Three)
Domain Manager	*Olof*	*Me*	*Me*
International trips	Olof	Me	Me
Domestic vacations	Olof	Me	Me
Weekend couple getaways	Olof	--	--
Car trips	Olof	Me	Me
Ski trips	Olof	Me	Me
Backpacking	Olof	--	--
Family cycling trips	Olof	--	--
Bike maintenance	Olof	Friends	Friends
Running/marathon support	Olof	Me	Me
Picnics	Me	--	Me
Extended family visits	Me	Me	Me

FAMILY CALENDAR & TRADITIONS	(Before)	(Year One)	(Year Three)
Domain Manager	**Olof**	**Me**	**Me**
Plan social activities	Me	Me	Me
Arrange extracurriculars	Me	EN	EN
Weekend agenda	Me	Me	Me
Plan birthday parties	Me	Me	Me
Gifts for girls	Me	Me	Me
Gifts for extended family	Me	Me	Me
Tending holiday traditions	Me	Me	Me
Christmas cards	Me	--	Me
Christmas tree excursion	Olof	Me & Friends	Me
Christmas house lights	Olof	Helper	Helper
Holiday meals	Me	Me	Me
Pumpkin carving	Olof	--	--
Easter egg dying	Olof	--	--
Fireworks	Olof	--	--
Holiday decorating	Me	--	Me

CARS	(Before)	(Year One)	(Year Three)
Domain Manager	**Olof**	**Me**	**Me**
Driving	Olof	Me	Me
Car purchase	Olof	Me	Me
Car maintenance	Olof	Me	Me
Car insurance	Olof	Me	Me

 McKay Moore Sohlberg

PETS	(Before)	(Year One)	(Year Three)
Domain Manager	*Olof*	*Me*	*Me*
Feeding	Olof & Girls	Me	Me
Vet visits	Olof	--	Me
Pee, poop, barf	Olof & Girls	Helper	Helper

FAMILY EMOTIONAL HEALTH	(Before)	(Year One)	(Year Three)
Domain Manager	*Me*	*Me*	*Me*
Soothing girls' hurt feelings	Me	Me	Me
Relationship consult	Me	Me	Me
Parent angst support	Olof	Me	Me
Family humor & fun	Olof & Me	--	Me
Sex education, etc.	Olof & Me	EN	EN

MEDICAL	(Before)	(Year One)	(Year Three)
Domain Manager	*Olof*	*Me*	*Me*
Family doctor appts.	Olof & Me	Me	Me
Health insurance	Olof	Me	Me
Wounds, medication, etc.	Olof	Me	Me

ENTERTAINMENT	(Before)	(Year One)	(Year Three)
Domain Manager	**Me**	**--**	**Me**
Planning	Me	--	--
TV show/using remote	Olof	--	Me
Buying tickets online	Olof	--	--
Reading movie/book reviews	Olof & Me	--	Me

COMMUNITY ENGAGEMENT	(Before)	(Year One)	(Year Three)
Domain Manager	**Olof**	**--**	**Me**
Supporting political causes	Olof	--	Me
Reading & distilling the news	Olof	--	Me
Letters to the editor	Olof	--	--
Charitable giving	Olof & Me	Me	Me
Community volunteer work	Olof & Me	--	--

CHURCH	(Before)	(Year One)	(Year Three)
Domain Manager	**Me**	**Me**	**Me**
Motivator	Me	Me	Me
Sunday School teacher	Me	Me	EN
Vestry	Olof	--	--
Infusing in everyday life	Olof & Me	Me	Me

   McKay Moore Sohlberg

As I set out to plug the holes in the dike, I identified fourteen major life domains that encompassed the bulk of our family life. It seemed that Olof was responsible for about seven domains, which encompassed about forty-two subtasks. When he died, these tasks had to be abandoned, delegated, or learned. The process of redistributing the tasks of living is layered. Initially it was an acute, but constant, and horrifically scary, reminder that he was gone, and I was now the solo head of the household. A few tasks felt particularly onerous, as I had so little practice. Take for example, cars. I remember a few months after Olof died, I was leaving my counseling appointment and somehow managed to hook the bumper of my car, a vehicle that Olof had researched and purchased, on the parking lot rail. It made a terrible noise as I backed away. Instead of stopping to assess the damage to the car, I just kept driving. I knew that inspection would offer nothing, as I had no knowledge of how to assess or respond to whatever damage I might find. I even stopped to complete an errand on the way home. The car was drivable, so I pressed on. I was buying time, as I wasn't sure what my next move should be. When I got home, I sat paralyzed in the parked car in my driveway. Olof would have gauged the level of damage, called the insurance company, and let me know what to do in order to address the situation. Are you supposed to call the insurance company before you have the car looked at by an auto body shop, or do you take it to the car folks before you call the insurance company? Either way, who were the contacts and what were the phone numbers for the insurance company and auto body shop? Perhaps the damage was not extensive enough to warrant an insurance report, but how does one judge this? I tried to remember what Olof had done in the past when the girls had scraped the car. But I couldn't. I embarrassedly asked a friend to look at the car. He got on his back and scooted under the front of the car. When he emerged, he shook his head and said, "Sorry. This is going to cost you—call the insurance company, and they'll tell you what to do."

At some level, the demands of taking on new roles served as a distracter and perhaps held some of the deepest, immobilizing pain at bay. I could not fold and give in to my fear and grief because there were very real responsibilities that took all my cognitive and emotional effort to tend. The process was also in part therapeutic, as it facilitated the identity reconstruction that ultimately would need to occur in order for me to heal. I didn't know it then, but the fight to get my feet on the ground kept me moving forward. Years later, there are tasks that I have not yet mastered that remain on the "to learn" list. For example, I am determined to learn how to independently turn on my TV, stream movies, and record programs. In the years after Olof died, I did not even try to turn on the TV. I cleverly held soup parties during the presidential debates and made myself busy in the kitchen while someone went to operate the mysterious "universal remote" that magically turns the TV to the right channel. As I write this chapter, I am reclaiming some activities and adding new ones. With help from friends like Rob, garden chores such as taking care of the raspberries feel less daunting. He built the trellis, I purchased the vines, and come summer, I will be ready to harvest. I look forward to a time when I can independently pack my backpack and embark on a wilderness adventure, as I've missed this activity. What is nice is that I now believe I can learn these tasks when the time is afforded. Some of the smallest feats have given me the greatest sense of accomplishment. I love that I have learned how to BBQ a couple of items and can have friends over. Don't ask me why, but it makes me feel hip to chat with my friends while at the grill. I also like that I can have a reasonably astute conversation about the pros and cons of different models of SUV hybrid cars. These skills were not in my repertoire two years ago. There are, however, some tasks that I simply am not going to master because I don't have the inclination. I need my attorney, accountant, and financial planner and have learned just enough to use them wisely. Then there's the hopeful glimmer of novel tasks. Thanks to mentorship from friends like the Boyds and Karen who share a passion for nature, I witness myself gaining skills that are newcomers to my list. Indeed, I'm becoming a bird-watcher and a mushroom gatherer.

Tasks are not just items on a to-do list to help you have a successful week or achieve your family goals. The ways in which families or individuals structure and prioritize their life tasks gives them a daily, weekly, and even seasonal rhythm. That has been a very difficult aspect of the widowhood process. For example, after the girls got older and more independent, our Saturdays had a predictable, special couple's cadence. We'd usually putter in the garden or do house chores after our respective morning run and bike ride, which almost always concluded with a sixteen-ounce, 2 percent chocolate latte from Full City Coffee. Then we'd run around town and do the Saturday errands in the car together. He drove while I marked things off the list. I still miss Saturdays.

Crying and Other Phenomena of Mood

Changing Moods

In Oregon we embrace the saying, "If you don't like the weather, just wait five minutes." It felt like my unpredictable moods mocked me as they mirrored the fickleness of the Northwest climate. Take today. It's a fall Saturday, and it has been two years and four months since Olof's death. I woke up to a glorious, sunny morning made particularly brilliant after a couple of days of rain. I pulled my bedroom curtains, and the world sparkled. I waited to see if my psyche would embrace the beauty, and I'd start out with a positive anticipation of the day, or whether I'd feel sad that the house was quiet and there was no Olof to share this pretty Saturday. My mood landed somewhere in between, and I began to plan my day, which was uncharacteristically free from a schedule. Emma had just left to start her junior year at the University of Michigan, and although Ericka was in Eugene for an internal medicine rotation at our local hospital, she was working long hours and would not be home till later. Tatum had returned to her job in California after a weekend visit to show her boyfriend her childhood home. Even my running mates were out of town, so my usual Saturday run would be solo and could be executed when it suited me.

The world was my oyster. I made myself a latte and contemplated the view of the Coburg Hills from the picture window in our kitchen. To my surprise, I started crying. Trigger? Not sure. A deep, melancholy ache seemed to have been ignited by the beauty of the day. I had learned how to let the sadness come, however uninvited. No need to suppress it this morning. I had time and privacy.

I reflected on the last few weeks, which had been full of family visits. Erika and Michael, my sister and brother, had come to Eugene, and we had enjoyed a sibling fest. We talked openly about my healing and where I felt stalled. Mostly we just enjoyed being together in the way that only siblings can relate. We laughed about childhood and shared family gossip. All three girls had been home, and together we enjoyed watching a cabaret that Emma had produced for our town with a repertoire of songs that made the theater audience members both laugh and cry. My parents had also been to Eugene. I was much more stable than in their previous visit, and I saw them relax. Emma, my parents, and I took a road trip to the Sohlberg cabin on Flathead Lake in Montana where we visited with Olof's family and let the Flathead magic take all our cares away. Summer had wound to a close, and the house was quiet.

As my tears dried, I began to feel grateful for family. Olof's death had forced me to rely on extended family and deepened my relationships. Suddenly, I realized that I was feeling happy. But not for long. I was just like a mad toddler sitting in a stroller, wailing and red faced until the howls shift tenor and the child begins to giggle, tears still wet on her cheeks. The parent cajoles the change in mood with a peekaboo game. I felt frustrated with having the emotional control of a two-year-old.

My cell phone buzzed with Tatum's ringtone. She was calling to solicit feedback on one of her medical school applications. We had a dynamic conversation as she reviewed her ideas and shared what she had been doing at the clinic where she worked. Her commitment to and interest in advancing the health of under-resourced communities was evident in her application essay and in her enthusiasm for her work. I had that wonderful feeling of parental satisfaction when you witness your child's competence. In one hour, my mood meter had jumped from the "contemplative" tick to the "sad" tick to the "happy" tick, then to the "frustrated tick," and now landed on the "proud" tick.

I tied my running shoes and set out to run the river loop on this beautiful morning. I warmed up by jogging slowly and then kept a steady pace for a few miles until I began to push myself. I felt strong. My moods are like my running—I cannot always anticipate or control how I will feel, but when I do feel good, it is oh-so-nice.

Waiting is its own mood and is one that I am finding has become prominent. I've never been skilled at living in the moment. I'm a planner, goal directed, and I like to make things happen. I have to work at being present. In my new life, I've had difficulty establishing a comfortable time referent. My previously prevailing focus on *future*, or what is next, no longer works the same. The future doesn't hold him, nor has it fully revealed new promises. The *present* requires a conscious effort to work at redefining my days,

 McKay Moore Sohlberg

as so many former routines are gone. I want so badly to at least celebrate the glorious *past*, but it is so disconnected with my present and future, I can't do it yet. The element of time that feels like the best fit is *waiting*. I think grieving people spend substantial time waiting for their next mood.

During days or hours when I'm feeling the beauty, the gratitude, and have a touch of grace, I realize that at some level, I'm waiting for the good feelings to recede and be replaced by loneliness or heartache. During episodes of dark, I've learned to take solace that it will pass and my changing moods will bring light.

A New Mood That I Wish Would Go Away

For me, regret is an insidious sentiment that formerly was not a big part of my mood repertoire. You don't have to be Freud to know this is a common challenge in suicide survivors. One workbook suggests the following journaling exercise: *"You will need to have courageous honesty to complete this assignment. Write a dialogue in which you express your regrets and include your loved one's response."* I execute that assignment in my head far more often than I think is useful.

Regret used to be such a benign word. "I can't make your party—regrets." It was part of my perennial parent warnings: "If you don't wear your retainer, you'll regret it because your pretty smile will be altered" or "Be nice to that annoying classmate, or you'll regret it, as she'll probably turn out to be your boss one day." Now, however, *regret* has a deeper, darker meaning. It even has an associated set of somatic symptoms characterized by a generalized contraction of my innards beginning with my throat and extending to my belly. Not to be overly dramatic, but I feel captive to regret.

The element of regret that enslaves me is this sense of despair about circumstances that I cannot change and my role in them. Why didn't I look up when I was in the shower that morning—when he popped in to say he had a flat tire on his bike and had come home for a new tube? I was in a hurry from my own morning run and late to work. I did not even look up. I missed my chance to look at his beautiful face one last time. I regret this.

Why didn't I pick up on hints that he was not feeling well? Why didn't I ever ask him if he was taking his medication and whether there were side effects? Why didn't I study bipolar disease when he was first diagnosed three decades ago? Why didn't I run upstairs as soon as I discovered the gun box? My unalterable list of *whys* tortures me.

Regret dialogues happen often in my head:

My Forgiving Self: *"You didn't know. No one did—it shocked everyone."*

My Regretful Self: *"But I am the one person who should have monitored how he was doing."*

My Forgiving Self: *"He needed to ask you for help."*

My Regretful Self: *"I didn't give him room to ask me because he was so invincible and capable. I didn't allow him to be human."*

My Forgiving Self: *"He was diagnosed when he was an adolescent, before there was treatment. He lived a magnificent life. Neither he nor you understood his vulnerability. That was part of his disease."*

My Regretful Self: *"But the books say there are almost always signs."*

My most painful regrets are not actually around his death. I think at some level, I am starting to believe that his disease took him. We both did what we could with cir-

 McKay Moore Sohlberg

cumstances beyond our control. As time goes by, I am more plagued by the everyday regrets. For not taking more time to smell the roses. For every dumb argument. For being bossy. For being angsty. For worrying about the small stuff. For not telling him over and over that he was an amazing husband, father, and friend. For not kissing him more. I want so many do-overs. But my Forgiving Self reminds me that we didn't live like we had limited time. The gloriousness of growing up together and sharing thirty-two rich years that resulted in our three amazing daughters speaks for itself. Be quiet, my Regretful Self.

Crying

About eight months after Olof died, I had a realization that not one day had passed that I hadn't cried. Mind you, they were not all sob fests. Some episodes were just short, salty, stinging sensations that left the mascara fully intact. Others involved the whole body and left me as spent as if I'd just pushed myself on a hard run. These could be an impressive symphony, each theme replete with racking sobs, howling, and a crescendo of snot. The final movement was always those involuntary hiccup-breaths with lengthening intervals that I associate with children getting over a tantrum.

I felt embarrassed and unnerved by my crying and looked for facts to normalize it. I read in a women's health magazine that women cry on average sixty-four times per year. While my crying was associated with understandable fragility, there was a nagging worry that it was an indicator I was somewhat unhinged. I read some more and was surprised to learn that some scientists believe that human beings are the only animals on the planet who cry in response to sadness. A comparative analysis on the chemical makeup of "emotional" versus "reflexive" tears (that is the soap-in-your-eye, peeling-onions brand of tears) suggests that the former has proteins and hormones that are not present in the latter. There is a strong suggestion in the popular science press that emotional crying serves to rid the body of certain stress chemicals, and that accounts for why people often feel better "after a good cry." I started to feel less worried and self-conscious about my "crying when sad" and tried to conceptualized it as therapeutic. There were times, however, when the tears came at inopportune times and knocked me back to a state of embarrassment and insecurity.

It was around the two-year mark in my grief timeline, and I was no longer carrying around little tissue packs for surprise tears. I went to see my accountant to sign my tax returns. Taxes represented one of those domains that I had worked hard to understand. I was feeling relatively triumphant that this year I had independently got all my materials together and mostly understood the purpose of the papers and forms. I had scheduled an early morning appointment to sign my returns at the accountant's office. The meeting around the oval oak table was going smoothly. I understood what I was signing, had brought the proper checks made out to the proper entities, and had even asked a few reasonable questions and understood the answers.

My accountant is a family friend, and after we completed our business, we took a few moments to catch up on our children. Then out of the blue, it hit me like a ton of bricks—Olof was gone. I was signing tax returns as a single person, sitting in the office where Olof had organized our joint filing and brought home the returns for me to sign and then brought them back to this room. I lost it. It was sort

 McKay Moore Sohlberg

of like that moment when you can no longer fight nausea and you vomit. A physiologic event that is not to be quelled or postponed. I started crying, *really crying*. There was no tissue on the large round oak table, and my only choice was my sweater sleeve, which I might have been able to use somewhat discretely if it had not been navy blue. The glistening white snail trails were well highlighted on the contrasting dark surface. I tried to get a grip but simply could not stop crying. My heart was broken, and it did not care that it was not a convenient time. My accountant was nothing but kind and compassionate, but even years later, the memory makes me cringe. Crying in professional spaces violates societal politesse. I had so wanted to leave that tax meeting feeling successful and competent.

It felt like there were so many triggers where my response was to cry. I cried out of frustration when I could not open a jar or zip up my dress and just wanted Olof to be there to carry out his husbandly duties. I cried with loneliness when I watched the girls perform or receive recognition and honors and wanted Olof to share my pride. I've cried with jealousy when friends celebrated their thirtieth anniversary, as we didn't make it that far. I think the common thread behind all the triggers was the longing for something that had previously been mine. A child might cry over the loss of an ice-cream cone that topples to the ground. I cried over not having Olof to share my empty nest years. Humans have the capacity to dwell on the "if onlys" and "how comes?" Tears are our response to life's inevitable unfairness, and as uncomfortable as crying has been, I think my tears helped me seek equilibrium.

One context that supported therapeutic crying was the shower. It is private. Tears and mucus are easily rinsed away. The cleansing metaphor also worked for me, as I felt like I could wash away the sadness for a time. For many months, my morning shower was a meditative, ritualized cry.

Thank God for Imagination

Crying is not the only therapeutic activity available to the bereft. Imagination provides another comfort-bearing option. In the same way that humans appear to be uniquely wired to cry for sadness, I think they are also programmed with a capacity to creatively connect with realms that are beyond their physical observation. I am not a believer in the angel-on-the-cloud concept, but the fact that we can conjure up this and related images makes me believe that we are meant to tap this creative imaging in order to incorporate death into our life, and it is an antidote to the sadness. Some might call this faith. All of us will die, and before we do so, we will all be affected by death. I appreciate God's gifts of crying and imagination. I like to imagine that Olof, or some semblance of his soul, can sense my thoughts. It has allowed me to reassure him, thank him, ask him why, and tell him how much it hurts. Sometimes he even answers me back.

Please, God, Just One Afternoon

I think it would start by me taking a nap and you materializing in our bed with me tucked around you, head on your chest just so, our sleeping position for over three decades. We'd look at each other, and it would feel natural, familiar, and just right. I loved how comfortable

     McKay Moore Sohlberg

we were. Best friend. Soul mate. Father of our children. Listener to all my angsts. None of these do us justice, but you know what I mean.

We don't have time for reviewing the petty, inevitable concerns born out of the demands of growing up together, raising children, and pursuing demanding careers. We would distill our messages to the important content that we each ache to tell the other. I believe you would try to reassure me that I was not at fault. You would insist on taking responsibility for your actions and maybe try to explain the disease a bit more fully and give me answers to the glaring questions. I would remind you that we were a partnership like no other, and that I needed to give you more room and space to express fears and insecurities and admit you were powerless. I needed to pay more attention to your vulnerabilities. We would cry, yearn, and forgive.

Then would start our celebration. You'd praise my motherhood, my support of you in hard times, and you'd help me remember the zillion special times. You'd remind me that I was smart, fun, and adventurous and that you found me pretty, strong, and loved being with me every second. I'd thank you for your unconditional love of me and the girls, your capacity to do whatever we needed, and the endless gifts teaching us how to strive for social justice, condition our bodies, enjoy the outdoors, and take care of our friends and family. I would tell you how adorable and funny you were from Day 1 and that I was so proud of being your wife. I'd tell you that you were a sexy surgeon, and people were jealous of me for having it all, and they were right to feel so.

We'd spend most of our time talking about the girls. We'd revel. We'd reminisce. We'd dream. I'd worry a bit and you'd reassure.

At some point, it would be time to go. I want to write that it'd be okay and that somehow we'd find peace from the gift of an afternoon. That you would reassure me that there's unimaginable gloriousness in life beyond that transcends all earthly concerns. That I could convince you that you gave us sufficient tools and means to carry forward and that you are instilled deep in our souls. Please, God, just one more afternoon.

Navigating Ashes, Closets, and Other Uncharted Waters

Death is one of life's greatest mysteries. It's inevitability is a source of wonder, fear, and perplexity across time and cultures. However, in spite of its ubiquity, navigating the aftermath of death in our society sorely lacks procedural road maps and is fraught with lonely decisions that leave one feeling isolated from the "living world." In the early days, I found myself longing for the traditional, simple attitudes toward death that I saw depicted in movies and books of ages past when death seemed normalized and marked by predictable patterns of meaningful ceremony. I've thought a lot about this, and I think the characteristic that these traditional cultures display around death that makes me feel the most wistful is their openness.

Death simply is not polite in our society. A curious fact since it will happen to us all. Case in point, death talk is usually a conversation stopper.

"Did you come to the conference this year with your husband?"

"No, he actually passed away in April."

"Oh, umm, I'm so sorry. Ummm. Well, running late to my talk. See you at dinner."

What else was she supposed to say when the subject is so taboo? If she asked me further questions, she might be viewed as prying. If she asked me how I'm doing, she might worry I'd become unwantedly upset in a professional setting.

During the initial months following Olof's death, I occasionally experienced worried, furtive glances in the supermarket or espresso line from well-meaning acquaintances who I believe wanted to approach me and express condolences but were not sure what to say. I noticed them become very focused on their broccoli selection or on evaluating the artistry of the foam design in their latte in order to avoid eye contact and possible speaking obligation. There were others who were risk-takers and perhaps lacked a bit of social restraint who came right up and dove into the personal well beyond our relationship, but were just trying to do the right thing. Wouldn't it be nice if we had some type of ritualized, open acknowledgment that took away the burden of feeling afraid you might offend or upset someone? If I were in charge of politesse, I would institute some version of *"Blessings on his spirit and healing to all who feel pain"* when someone shares they have lost someone. If I get my courage up, I'm going to try that out on someone who has lost a spouse. I think it might feel nice to both of

     McKay Moore Sohlberg

us. I might feel like I offered some comfort, and the other person might feel less lonely.

In our culture, you just sort of make up death management as you go. If the death is sudden, and the person is not of an expected age, you have a lot of decisions, but also a lot of latitude, for how you will handle the unmentionables. Funerals, memorial services, the body, notifying people, and your public persona involve a huge menu of complicated choices that alienate you from your previous cushy world of death naiveté. In retrospect, I feel grateful for three circumstances that helped me make important death decisions and kept some semblance of connection to my previous self. First, I was surrounded by very close friends and family who took my cue that I needed openness around Olof's suicide and wanted his life fully honored. Second, I live in a relatively small community that is characterized by social responsibility and caring for the unfortunate. Thank you, Eugene. There were times when I wanted to be anonymous, but in retrospect, I'm glad you didn't allow that. Third, and most important, I am a mother to three daughters, whose own resilience and trust in me brought clarity to most decisions I needed to make. Still, it was hard and exhausting.

Ashes are no longer restricted to campfires.

If you walk in our (now, my) bedroom, there is a simple, but elegant square box made from beautiful cherry wood sitting on my grandmother's marble table. It is an urn that holds Olof's ashes. A lot of decisions were made to get to the point of having that urn in my bedroom, some under tremendous duress. Even two and a half years later, I get this strangely surreal, disconnected feeling when I remember that I am a person who has an urn in her bedroom to store her Beloved's ashes.

I remember going to the mortuary to select the urn. It was not unlike going to Nordstrom and having a personal shopper. There was a very nice, knowledgeable person ushering me through the showroom, describing the urn options lined up neatly on display shelves in an attempt to help me identify an honorable receptacle to match my stated taste. I was so shocked by the breadth of inventory that I could not focus on the details of selection. I remember one urn that was a ceramic golf village replete with a smiling golfer fully clad in traditional Scottish plaid. He was surrounded by a caddy and some adoring onlookers as he was positioned to swing his glazed golf club to connect with the tiny ceramic ball onto the shiny ceramic green in anticipation of a hole in one. The top of the clubhouse had a chimney with a removable plug, which I could only imagine was for retrieving (inserting?) the ashes. There was a cheesy message on the grand, glazed double doors of the clubhouse structure that said something about a life well lived. I kept wondering if anyone other than Tiger Woods or his successors would welcome having their life summed up by one hobby, even if it was a passion. Unfortunately, the sales tour went downhill from there. Next, I became fixated on a shelf of urns where you could store your Beloved's ashes in the same vessel as those of a family pet. I kept thinking of how many times Olof and I had joked about clandestine methods to ease Tatum's cat, Hermione, to the World Beyond after Tatum left for college and Hermione began peeing in the house. Maybe Olof would think it was hilarious and a private joke between the two of us. Ultimately, however, I

     McKay Moore Sohlberg

maintained my decorum and found what would best suit storage of his remains. A solid, hardwood geometric block with clean lines and a natural sheen. I weakly pointed to my selection and walked out to my car.

Deciding to cremate your fifty-one-year-old husband and store his ashes in an urn in your home is among your first decisions. But following through with your decisions requires responses in yet more uncharted territory. When the cremation has been completed, and it is time to procure your urn with ashes, you have to pick them up and drive them home. I could not help thinking that the project was not unlike picking up dry cleaning after it was ready. I just couldn't make myself do it as if I were carrying out a usual errand. I called our minister from the mortuary parking lot and asked him if I could drive straight to church in order for him to bless Olof's ashes before I brought them home. Mind you, this is not a usual sacrament or request. I do love our church. Father Bingham did not miss a beat and was agreeable to my homegrown request for an on-the-spot ritual. I drove midweek to the church Olof and I had attended for two decades of Sundays, walked inside holding my cherry urn, and met Father Bingham, who was waiting for me in the chapel. He gave a short blessing, and I walked out and buckled myself and Olof in the front seat and set off for home to find a spot to store his now blessed ashes. Since there was no customary practice, I got to make one up.

I want to write the lecture for Ashes 101 for those who are new to death management. Actually, I really want to write a yellow-and-black clad volume of *Death for Dummies*. If I would have had some warning or tips for how to manage the myriad practical and emotional issues that come with the territory, I think I would have been spared some major angst. Let's begin with the emotional. I struggled initially to figure out what I wanted to do with his remains. I kept thinking about Ash Wednesday when the priest says, *"Remember you are dust and to dust you shall return."* It seemed so prophetic and inconceivable that I was living that at age fifty-one. What the heck was my plan for Olof's "dust"? I could store his ashes indefinitely and make an altar of respect somewhere in the house. That seemed like a reasonable option, but I felt like it was overly public and would be uncomfortable for people entering our home. I could spread them ceremonially in a place of significance. Also reasonable, but there was no *single* place more important than the others. The girls and I had a need to honor and memorialize Olof and recognize the richness of his life. Distributing ashes in different places of significance felt more right, and that is what we have been doing over the years.

I purchased a smaller urn that the mortuary filled, and the first distribution went to Flathead Lake, the home of the Sohlberg sacred family cabin. Early on, our friends Reed and Tina, with whom we had raised our daughters side by side, honored my request and took some ashes to Italy and spread them during the bike trip that we had been scheduled to take with them the fall after Olof died. They completed the trip that Olof had helped plan and came back with a lovely story about a rigorous hill climb he would have loved that preceded a summit that coincidentally had a statue of a saint and a nice vista where they sent Olof to the wind. I took some ashes to France and spread them in the rough Brittany seas where Olof and I and the girls had vacationed with my sister and family. I sprinkled another baggie of ashes outside the tent on a safari in South Africa where Tatum and Ericka and I had returned in remembrance of when Olof had led us on a similar African journey. One particularly poignant ashes distribution was watching Emma place a tiny, ceramic pot with matching cover containing her Daddy's ashes on her freshman dorm-room shelf. She was beginning college across the country only four months after her father had died. She was the last person who got to talk to him. I'll never forget helping her unpack and decorate her room, and watching her position the little pot that I had found at Eugene's Saturday Market resolutely, but proudly, on her bookshelf, where only she knew what it contained. Olof is in our garden, on Eugene's hillsides, at Stanford outside the church where we were married, on a favorite ski run at Snowbowl, and in a columbarium at our church. He has returned to the earth of three countries, and I personally delivered him to three continents, which marked special places we had been together. In all cases, people who loved Olof deeply memorialized him privately or in groups. Our dear friend Fariborz confessed to me on an ashes outing up Eugene's Mount Pisgah that he didn't spread his packet and instead took the ashes home. I love that. Some of the rituals were very sad, some were even fun, but in all cases, it felt right. The girls and I just made it up as we went. I believe our open acts of celebration have helped us and others heal. Death, even when it is by suicide, does not preclude celebrating the greatness of the life. Ashes to ashes and dust to dust. We will all be there someday.

There is a practical side to managing ashes. I'm not sure why this is a kept secret. If you want to disburse them, you have to open the urn. And there are no instructions. The first time I went to open the urn in order to bring ashes with me on a trip, I ran into a snafu from step one. There were a series of screws on the bottom that required me to find and operate a screwdriver. (See chapter 3—screwdrivers were on his list of duties.) The screwdrivers that I found in Olof's toolbox were not the kind with a cross. (I can never remember which one was given the name of Phillip.) I was very nervous and upset, which did not help the efficiency of my search through the garage. I fumbled around and finally located the screwdriver and went back to the privacy of my bathroom and began to open the urn. There, next to my toothbrush holder and makeup mirror, I began my project. Surreal. What would I find? I took off the cover and found ten large stacked plastic packets full of whitish ash. It was only then that I remembered that I had instructed the mortician to divide the ashes in packets to make them easier to distribute. Shock and denial can make a person very level headed.

I was rather horrified by how abundant the ashes were. That urn was full. Now I had the issue of needing to handle them in order to transfer the ashes to my tiny ziplock bag. I discovered that the little jewelry ziplock bags work well for transporting distribution portions of ash; thus, I'd procured a set. However, my teaspoon was too shallow, and I inadvertently made a mess. Do you rinse the spilled ashes down the sink? I did, but it bothered me. I then found a deep spoon used to measure cough syrup. Like Olof always said, *Find the right tool for the job, and the job will complete itself.* Easy for you to say, Mister Surgeon. My concentration was suddenly interrupted when I heard a friend call to me downstairs who had dropped by to check on things. What to say? I was in the

     McKay Moore Sohlberg

midst of a very intimate and private undertaking, and one that I knew would be upsetting to others. I could hardly shout out, *"Just a minute, don't come up, I'm busy spooning Olof's ashes into this jewelry bag so I can take him with me on the plane."* I stopped midstream and went downstairs to gracefully dismiss my friend, who inquired what I'd been working on. *"You have dust all over your shirt." "Oh, just dealing with some of Olof's garage tools."* Please don't notice my puffy eyes and shaky voice and ask more questions. Eventually my task was complete. My first urn opening.

Although other openings were less traumatic and done with more finesse, they continued to hold an element of horror. I blame our culture for this. You feel that you are doing something morbid and shameful, yet that is what you must do if you are disbursing ashes. One particular ashes-opening changed this. When I opened the urn and spooned out his precious ashes, I found a staple. Befuddled, I pondered the square staple for a long time. I decided it was likely a staple that he had in his collar bone from a ski accident, but I'm not totally sure. I tried to make friends with the staple—it was part of our memories. I remembered when he fell on that steep mogul run when we were home visiting family in Missoula and skiing at the local ski area. We were having so much fun—especially with his dad, Steve, who loved skiing more than any human being has ever loved a sport. I smiled remembering Olof's calm and friendly nature, no matter the situation. In spite of his pain and the struggle the ski patrol experienced when trying to load him on a sled perched on a very steep incline, he engaged them in talk about their jobs and the snow conditions. Olof was the type of person who made others' lives easier. I loved that about him and still do. This reverie led me to a nostalgic vision of what he looked like when he skied. He was an aggressive, fast but beautiful skier, and fun to watch. Then I thought about how Tatum particularly looks like him when she skis, and how he passed on his love of and athleticism for pursuing this sport to all three girls. Suddenly, the revulsion of finding the staple passed, and it seemed pleasant to be handling a physical part of Olof. Too bad, Western Civilization. Ashes are nice.

In summary, I offer you, the reader, some tips for ashes management:

Gather the right tools: Phillips screwdriver, ziplock jewelry bags, medicine spoon. Note: An alternative to ziplock bags are the plastic, screw-top pill boxes available at REI in several sizes. A coffee scoop also works if you are short on medicine spoons. Your choice.

Prepare yourself: The ashes are plentiful and more dense than you might imagine. They are lighter in color than you think and uneven in texture. You can see fragments that are bone that are different from the soft ashes. The ashes are messy. Best to transfer near a sink.

When Disbursing in Water: Because the ashes comprise different textures and weights, the substances behave differently. Some parts will sink immediately. Some will spread out and lie on the surface of the water for a long time. This is nice as you reminisce.

When Disbursing in Wind: Toss them in the direction the wind is blowing. Otherwise they will, for sure, come back in your face. If you forget, it's not the end of the world because they don't taste that bad.

     McKay Moore Sohlberg

The Three Hs

My experience with the ashes led me to the Three Hs when navigating the unspeakable death tasks that felt awkward at best and humiliating or horrifying at worst:

Head High

Honor Him

Humor Helps

The three Hs became a guidepost for how to manage interactions about Olof's death. Looking people in the eye and using my "loud, proud voice" was stabilizing, even when on the inside I played mind games about people's probable misperceptions or judgments. I was very quick to remind folks that Olof had left us well loved, which gave us strength. It was true, but it also let people know that his goodness was a safe and desired topic.

There are a lot of natural questions that people ask that could be difficult. Particularly when the cause of death is suicide. I always tried to remember that it would be worse if people didn't say what they were thinking or ignored me. The Three Hs helped me navigate dialogues that might otherwise have gone sideways and left me sad or bitter and caused the other person to feel uncomfortable.

> *"Are you going to stay in your house?"* [the imagined subtext was…"after all he died there"]
>
> Head High—smile, square up to the person, and validate the fact someone cares what happens to you.
>
> *"I appreciate your concern, and I'm sure a lot of people wonder about this…"*

Honor Him—remind them that his death did not change the wonderful life we shared together.

"The house actually feels really good to us. We have a lifetime of memories, and it helps us feel close to Olof."

Humor Helps—depending upon your relationship with the person, you can say it aloud or just in your head. (I easily amuse myself, so I often have numerous options that I admit lean toward the sarcastic.)

"Homelessness seems like a poor alternative" or *"If it doesn't work out, can we live with you?"* or *"We'll probably stay here until we join him."*

Closets Store More Than Clothes

Here's a another death topic that requires making practical decisions, steeped in emotional duress, and for which there are no road maps. Closets. I never realized how personal a closet is. There is something about a person's clothes and the items they stuff in a junk drawer that is very intimate. Olof had a walk-in closet, and, in general, it was pretty organized. The hanging rods held his work shirts, casual shirts, slacks, casual pants, tie rack, sports coats, and white lab coats in defined sections. The girls and I never really talked about it, but after he died, we independently had a practice of "visiting" the closet and looking through his things. There were some items that were traumatic for me to visit in the initial months—his glasses, his wallet, his pj bottoms that matched mine, and the Hutch's cycling jersey that I found sweaty and wadded up from his morning ride on the fateful day.

Other things were comforting from the beginning—I liked to look through his bazillion T-shirts. He was a T-shirt guy, and they marked our trips, his college days, his love of Montana, and his democratic political ideals. I would run my hands through all the medals marking triathlons, marathons, half marathons, and cycling races so that they would clink. He had a drawer full of cards that the girls and I had written him. I even found the anniversary card I had written on our very first anniversary. He had carefully stored every handmade Father's Day and birthday card. He so loved being their Daddy. I found trip journals in which he had catalogued some of our adventures. Even now, the cards are among my most valued treasures. They help me remember how much adoration he had received and give me hope that he left this world knowing how much we loved him.

What to do with the closet is another one of those very individual death management tasks that is full of decisions. I was talking to one of the girls' college friends who told me that she and her mom cleaned out her dad's stuff the week he died because it was just too painful to face his items with him gone. I can see where that might feel necessary. Some people elect to never clean out the closet. My tactic has been somewhere in between. My sister stayed with Emma and me in the weeks following Olof's death. With my input, she took everything out of his closet and dressers and then put it all back—perfectly. It looked like a magazine closet. I got to touch and look at everything. It was a way of preserving him, and I've liked having this space. It has evolved over time with some items leaving and some being added. Ericka's boyfriend, Lee, has done some shoe and tie shopping in the closet, which I have loved. He even took

Olof's blue blazer and wore it as best man in his brother's wedding. A few of my own items have found their way into his space as well. He has more room for my boots. (I like boots.) I am close to feeling ready to store his belongings now, which I think is a sign that I'm internalizing him and not needing the tangible reminders.

Once again, the Three Hs were useful—I held my head high as I distributed a few items to friends, believing they would appreciate something personal and not feel squeamish. I followed my instincts to honor him. I wrote him one last anniversary card since technically we had been together most of Year Twenty-Eight, and I added it to the closet collection. I teased Olof's spirit as I moved the vacuum to a spot front and center in the closet since it had irked him that it got stored in his closet and not mine. Humor helps.

Traditions—Dogma or Opportunity?

Holidays following a death require a lot of decisions—especially during the initial years. We are a family with well-established traditions that bring meaning and festivity to the seasons but highlight loss when a family member dies and can no longer perform his part in the ceremonies. We spent the first Thanksgiving with Olof's clan at his brother's house. The image of his three siblings and their children playing a board game around a table with their collective Swedish likeness, laughing at the funny quips and mutual teasing that is only possible when you share DNA and a common childhood, still evokes an indescribable pain. He loved his family so. My despair that he was missing this occasion, and would miss all those to come, led to a periodic need to slink into the haven of the bathroom so I could vomit. My guts knew the depth of this sadness. How can we have a family Thanksgiving without him?

Then came Christmas. I suppose some might criticize that our family had a ridiculously scripted Christmas holiday. My therapist had gently hinted that our merrymaking might be a bit rigid. However, it worked well for us. The white outdoor Christmas lights that outline the roofline, doors, and windows on both stories of our Dutch Colonial home evoked the same discussion (OK, argument) every year. I nagged Olof to hire someone to put up the lights out of fear he would kill himself when he fell off the roof (I know, ironic). He put them up anyway. After the house lights were up, we moved on to the tree procurement outing. We frequented the same U-cut Christmas tree lot, Northern Lights, and took a tractor ride out to where the grand firs are planted to locate our perfect tree. Olof was in charge of sawing down the tree and loading it on the tractor while the girls and I "helped," but inevitably we abandoned him early to return to the stand where they sold hot cider. When the girls started going to college, the remaining sister(s) would text photos of tree options so that we still operated using consensus for choosing the tree.

Once the tree was safely home, decorating ensued. Each girl had her personal collection to decorate the house (Ericka—Fabriche Santas, Tatum—Snowbabies, and Emma—Department 56 village). Olof would begin the tree trimming by putting the lights on the tree, followed by the gold ornaments, an annual gift from his grandmother. For some reason, he liked to hang them up high—I never asked, but maybe it stemmed from when the girls were little and liked to take off the ornaments and play with them. Then we would all chip in hanging the rest of the ornaments and retell the stories that go along with them. There would be some bartering to place favorite ornaments in more prominent positions. The handmade preschool ornaments with the girls' pictures triggered more vigorous bickering as each wanted to see her handprint-framed photo marking her childhood. The last ornament placed was the treetop angel. Olof would lift the girl whose turn it was and she'd place it on top. Continuing on till today, there is a very clear three-year rotation for this angel placement that is not to be violated.

My job has always been to hang up our stockings, which were handknit by my Aunt Val. My whole extended family has these matching stockings. From when my parents and aunt and uncle were first married, every birth and marriage was sealed with a new stocking from Val, with the newcomer's name and birth year knit in red and green yarn. The end of our tree trimming was marked by a family dance to Amy Grant's "Tennessee Christmas," the first carol played in the house that season. Don't even remember how that got started.

And that's just the tree decorating. We still had the rest of the season to go. We had traditional parties—the Boettchers' Christmas Eve eve party; the Graebners' soup party, and our annual Mother-Daughter Christmas tea. They all signify Christmas. I'll spare you the whole script for Christmas morning, but you get the idea. Two Christmas morning traditions do warrant note, however. The morning always started with the girls clad in matching pajamas that Santa had left when we returned from Christmas Eve church service. Yes, even when they were big girls in their twenties. The morning ended with a song. Since early grade school, the girls would write their own lyrics to a Christmas tune that provided a review of the family highpoints of the

   McKay Moore Sohlberg

year. It was always funny and poignant and was the last Christmas gift of the morning.

So now what? Do you hang four or five stockings? Who will put up the lights? Should I go to a new tree lot to make it less painful? I believe we each pondered unsaid worries about whether Christmas would ever feel special again. That first Christmas, we decided to do *some* of the pre-Christmas traditions and to do Olof's jobs for him. (Head High. Honor Him.) We had decided that it would be too painful to be at home for Christmas, so we planned a ski trip, just the four of us, to a place where we had never been as a family—Telluride. We consciously began the task of introducing new traditions and merging them with the old. A spa treatment after a ski day is a very nice holiday tradition that we started and that Olof would have detested. New can be good. That first Christmas, we decided on no present exchange but stockings. I hung the matching stockings above the two queen beds in our ski resort hotel room and put Olof's stocking in a place of honor over the television (Humor Helps). Santa had brought four sets of thematic flannel pjs made from a ski print and put them out Christmas Eve. In the morning, we initiated a modified rendition of our stocking exchange.

The girls had been worried about filling my stocking, as that was always Olof's purview. Evidently, they had been texting each other during their fall quarters away at their colleges to plan their approach. Our Aunt Val stockings are relatively large as stockings go, so the girls were worried that the contents would not be sufficient to fill the stocking. They were all far away, and thus could not do a dry run. Consequently, they erred on the side of more items. I promise you, I had the stocking from Mecca. They filled it in the bathtub of the hotel room. It needed a bathtub. I still smile when I think of their excitement at watching me enjoy my first daughter-filled stocking. Traditions can morph. Before we left for the ski lift, they said they had one more surprise. They had written the annual song. Their first Christmas without their father, and they kept the tradition alive because it felt good. Dry eyed and earnest, they sang to me words set to the tune "Jolly Old Saint Nicholas." Several verses chronicled special family times shared in the early part of the year before Olof had died. Several verses documented a candid appreciation for my strength to carry on for them. Traditions can continue too.

A Cultural Revolution

Rituals bring rhythm and meaning to situations. They take the guesswork out of interactions. I've spent a fair amount of time in France, and I like that I know how to greet people by kissing on each cheek. It is clear. Here, there's that awkward time at the door when you are not sure if the visitor is a hugger, a kisser, a back patter, or a "hi only" kind of person. Not in Europe. There's protocol. Similarly in the Middle East. We have very close Iranian friends in Eugene and spend much time in this cultural family circle. I love it. I know how to greet and how to say goodbye. If you are leaving a gathering, you know it takes a bit longer because you go around and say goodbye to each person. You don't have to think, "Should I sneak out and just nod to the host?" It's explicit and clear. When we toast the meal at the Iranian table, family and friends know to clink glasses with *each person* while looking him or her *directly in the eye* (otherwise you clink again). In my not so humble opinion, these protocols are what are missing in our society around death.

 McKay Moore Sohlberg

We do have a few positive established death rituals, however. I think we do an excellent job around food. When someone dies, most people receive meals. Not only is the nutrition helpful, but the caring gesture reminds survivors that they are not alone. I also think we do a good job around condolence cards. I remember the day when I went to the mailbox, and for the first time since Olof died, there were no cards. It had been many months after he had died. I realized how lucky I had been and how helpful it was to have received an ongoing slew of supportive letters honoring our life.

We simply need more verbal and behavioral protocols for the survivors and everyone who interacts with them. If the death is traumatic and/or the people are young, some ritualized behavior would be even more helpful. Given my family's propensity for tradition, here's a few that are top of my list.

Verbal protocol: As discussed, we need to have a clear response when an acquaintance shares that someone they care about has died and you are not sure of the person's state or disposition. I'll just add that the *"Blessings on his spirit and healing to all who feel pain"* should be accompanied by looking the person in the eye and not averting your glance.

Sleep protocol: If someone loses their spouse and has shared a bed with him for over three decades, sleep will be an issue. Why not have a protocol? Emma slept with me initially, which was a very tender act and a memory that I still treasure. But eventually, she had to go to college, and I needed to cope. I had very good success with putting large pillows on Olof's side of the bed so it was weighted properly for me to snuggle against. My brain could be lulled into sleep because the sensory part of bed felt familiar. Wouldn't it be nice if we gave people large pillows and openly acknowledged, "Sleep might be hard, and perhaps this will help"?

Seating protocol: If you are used to going places as a couple, sitting is lonely. You no longer sit next to your spouse. Dinner parties, movies, lectures, tandem cycling, yoga mats—wherever you went together, when you resume the activity, it will be a friend or family person or even a stranger next to you instead of your beloved. It hurt that it was not Olof next to me. However, there were a number of times when people behaved in some way that helped quell the pain. They'd say some version of "I want to sit next to you tonight." I think we should make that a protocol. For the first year when a widow or widower goes somewhere, there could be a positive affirmation of wanting to be their seat partner. An amazing example of how a seating protocol helped me occurred when I returned to our 6:00 a.m. spin class that Olof and I had attended every Wednesday morning. For years we spun side by side and then went for a chocolate latte. It was a ritualized morning date. I attempted to go back to spin class a couple of months after he died, and while I was crying my way through the cycling session, the person next to me on "Olof's bike" left early. The instructor, Sheri, actually got off her teaching bike on the pedestal in the front of the studio, and finished teaching the class from the bike next to me. Sheri's act helped acknowledge the pain of the empty bike and eased the pain of resuming my activity. She spun next to me for the initial months whenever my neighbor bike was empty. Still makes me tear up.

Customized protocols: Some of the most comforting rituals are those that get laid down after the person dies. Almost instinctively, I found myself establishing routines that made me feel secure and grounded. They almost always involved a trusted friend, safe conversation, and shared food and drink. Early on, I would show up at the Marashis' house and grab

 McKay Moore Sohlberg

a stool at their gleaming marble kitchen island. I sat at the same spot each time, accepted "some bubbly," and dined on "the nibbles" while Karen and Fariborz asked how I was doing. We would all share our updates and feelings of loss over Olof. The ritualized connection quelled my sadness. I did not know then that my position at the kitchen stool would remain a sanctuary for the years to come.

Another important ritual was the *gin-and-tonics-with-death-talk* that got established with my dear friend John Boettcher. John is one of Olof's and my oldest and best friends in Eugene, and we've gone full circle in the death realm. His wife, Donna, died from cancer at thirty-eight, and Olof and I were very much part of her death and John's struggle to heal. John was my only close friend at the time who had a similar experience, and while his story was different, he understood death. This time the tables were turned, and it was me who needed counsel. He and Olof shared a very special connection, so John helped me feel close to Olof. John also found love and happiness again with Susan and so gave me hope that I would not always feel such deep despondence. Without a deliberate plan, our special talks became ritualized. We would sit in the same two chairs in my kitchen, he'd mix our G&Ts and ask me how I was doing, and we'd begin talking. He taught me to try not to work so hard to find answers and instead embrace the questions. He introduced the idea that sadness has a paradoxical way of making the world look beautiful. We processed and reprocessed how Olof could have become so desperate without our knowing it. John shared his imagined conversations with Olof at the river where Olof is on one bank in the world beyond, and John is on the bank of the living. He told me that he believed

Olof could make him understand what happened. These ritualized conversations were a big part of my healing. Plus drinking gin and tonics after dinner was fun.

The Upside

It would indeed improve all of our lives to have a culture more comfortable with Death and all Her Trappings. However, at the end of the day, grief will still require work, and not just on the part of the survivors. People with broken hearts are not the easiest folks to be around. Most of us bereaved souls know this. Although we wish not to be burdensome, if we survivors are to heal, we must confront our pain and figure out our new place in the world. Sometimes this means that those around us must walk a delicate tightrope adorned with eggshells. The same condolence statement might comfort us one day and hurt the next. We may appear hopeful, bitter, sad, inspired, wretched, and joyful, and it's not always clear what we need. We can be exhausting. Perhaps, though, there is an upside.

Lately I've been trying to give myself permission to believe the words of some of my closest friends and family who assure me that sharing my complicated grief journey has been a privilege. They claim that navigating the demanding roller coaster has deepened them and made their life richer. I guess I can believe their words since I have found that wrestling with my own emotions and trying to make sense of the insensible does have a transcendent quality. The phrase "there is no light without dark" pokes at my consciousness and soothes me. There's an uncomfortable tension, however, as I want to reject what feels like a Pollyanna narrative to make lemonade out of lemons, when the lemons are the tragic and violent death of my husband. I have to compromise and remind myself that, of course I would trade the lessons and the light for a chance to intervene and prevent Olof's death, but I can't, so I might as well try to celebrate what we had and garner the positives that do grow from tragedy. Everyone who loves Olof has been forced to feel the profundity that life has to offer. We don't get to choose the circumstance, but we can embrace the opportunities.

CHAPTER SIX

The Girls

I'm not sure I could have written this chapter without a few years of perspective under my belt. It simply would've been too scary. Giving voice to my fears might have somehow tipped the cosmic course for my deepest fears to come true. My dark night of the soul fears were haunting. The girls. *Would their sadness immobilize them into a state of depression? Would their healing be fraught with a protracted course of wayward choices as they dealt with anger, abandonment, and fear? Would they have difficulty forming healthy, intimate relationships?* And my worst, albeit most selfish fear, *Would they not want to come home to me because it would remind them of their pain?*

That very first night, we were forced to begin the process of grappling with the obliteration of our world as we knew it. We cloistered ourselves in the bedroom that Olof and I shared, and huddled together on our queen-sized bed that suddenly was big enough for four women. How would I support my bereaved, precious daughters, who were each on the brink of major life junctures? I remember feeling an odd surge of resolve sprinkled with a tiny bit of hope. Maybe it was the denial process kicking in—that magnificent psychological phenomenon that mitigates the horror of reality until we can cope. But I don't think that totally explained it. Even now, looking back, I had a sense of someone supporting me in my darkest hour. That first night was honestly one of the few times in my life that I felt divinely inspired. I heard myself confidently tell the girls that we would figure it out. We would carry on as Daddy had taught us. There would be dark times, but we were Sohlbergs, and we would navigate this and probably even transcend it. Above all, I promised them that they would be my forever priority, and I would have their backs and be their father and mother, and that I was up to the task. I assured them that Olof's love would endure and help sustain us. Yes, these were big promises, but at that moment, I knew I could keep them.

In some peculiar way, I was helped by channeling Olof's steadiness, a fact that may be hard for many to comprehend. Understandably, a layperson's view of suicide as an intentional decision means they must hold the person responsible for the ensuing pain and chaos. However, that particular interpretation was not, and still is not, a sentiment that I share. Not all suicides are alike. In our case, I do not believe that Olof's suicide was a rational choice, but an impulsive act in the midst of a rapid downward spiral—an unavoidable by-product of unfortunate brain chemistry that he had gallantly managed most of his life. I'm not trying to make excuses, but other than *that* day, he delivered. Especially on the husband and parenting front. He was a Steady Eddie and quelled my natural motherly angst as it arose. So I reached to the Olof within me, and to the Olof in the mysterious places beyond, to channel his guidance with the girls.

My reason for getting my head off my pillow every day and figuring it out was crystal clear. I felt an intense single-mindedness during those first few years. I can be pretty directed, but I had no idea how focused my being could become. That eye-on-the-prize, make-it-happen type of thinking burned within and drove my actions. I had never felt such singular drive. My children needed me.

Thank You, Mentors

I began where I usually begin when I need direction—reading research from experts. I looked for counsel from those who knew firsthand what my girls were facing, and then attempted to backward engineer our course to optimize the chance that they might avoid some of the pain and pitfalls described by those who had walked a similar road before them. I read several books with narratives by adults who had lost parents to suicide as adolescents and were still struggling in their middle-aged years. There were several themes that jumped out at me. First, there seemed to be a binary grouping. There were adults who had lost a parent as a youth and experienced difficulties because no one ever talked to them about their loss and their feelings. Their parent suicide was the elephant in the living room—not to be discussed. These survivors described how they were expected to carry on with their normal routines and were inadvertently taught that it was not okay to talk about the death of their parent. They learned to associate shame with the forced silence, and lived with a deep, dark secret locked inside. Many of these individuals had experienced trauma around the suicide, which added to their turmoil. This group ended up with repressed and unresolved issues that haunted them decades later.

     McKay Moore Sohlberg

There was a group at the other end of the continuum whose young lives were totally rearranged and all routines uprooted when the surviving parent collapsed and was unable to cope. These were people who suddenly not only had to deal with their own loss, but had added responsibility foisted on them as they needed to parent their remaining parent. These resilient adults described the loss of their childhood and the ensuing difficulties with emancipation and personal actualization. I'm grateful to all those who bravely shared their stories and pain and offered insights to me as a new parent of children coping with the suicide of a father they adored and upon whom they depended. In a sense, their model is the reason I am driven to write this chapter. Maybe my stories will help another parent.

I tried hard to consider the advice of the people in the stories I had read, and attempted to strike a balance between involving my girls in decisions and discussions, even when they were not comfortable and felt reticent, while trying to still protect them from the trauma and drama around their new identity. For example, I held Emma's lease money for her college group house hostage until she reported that she had shared her circumstances with her pending housemates. It felt important that, since she was far away from home with little overlap to her former life, she be authentic and not hide a large part of herself from those with whom she was establishing close friendships. It didn't take much prompting until she complied. Whether it made a difference for her, I don't really know. At the very least, however, it made us "talk about talking about *it*." There were some non-optional visits to a counselor, which were met with variable levels of engagement, but again, the process of talking and seeking help forced us to remain in dialogue and to learn about each other's individual needs and trajectories. As a parent, I refused to give into the very real stigma that accompanies suicide. We would keep talking.

I endeavored to share my grief at appropriate intervals with an appropriate level of disclosure, and I believe, was *mostly* successful. Sometimes my own needs got in the way, however. For example, I had a compulsion to make sure Olof was properly honored and remembered. This led me to quickly share a detailed *Olof tale* or *Olof memory* to friends, acquaintances, and yes, even strangers, in order to reinforce his goodness and preserve his presence. Sometimes this was helpful to the girls, but sometimes it was only nice for me. I know that my oversharing, TMI tendency was occasionally stressful and embarrassing to them. I would then deeply regret giving into my own neediness. I was hard on myself if I perceived that I hadn't gotten it right with the girls. Every conversation and action felt loaded and critical to their adjustment. In reality, however, I needn't have had my shorts in a constant knot. I could've trusted the girls a lot more. They were strong and solid in their love for their father, his love for them, and in their love for me, each other, and mine for them. There was plenty of room for mistakes for all of us. The foundation was established long before Olof's death and is called a *family*. I had to learn that his suicide did not change the family foundation. I had to learn that the *intent* to be facilitatory to their recovery was usually enough.

I lost my adult soul mate and had to face the pending empty nest solo. I was robbed of a phase that would've been our special couples' time and was grieving the loss of my chance to grow old with the one man I had loved. The girls lost their precious father, who had been a rock, a model, and a source of fun and adventure. He would miss every

     McKay Moore Sohlberg

important life juncture for them and would never see them on a professional stage, attend their college graduations, or walk them down the aisle. Both these parent and child realities are horrible and cannot be compared. In the end, though, I was the parent and needed to think hard about how to care for my girls who were still children in many respects. I was the most responsible party. I think that it was helpful to remember that. I had an inner mantra of "Remember, you are the parent." I let the girls participate in *some* of my grown-up despair and fear, and they always rose to the occasion to validate. I do not, however, think it was helpful for them to witness the prostrate, gasping for air moments, and mostly I did that solo or with a few close friends or family. Occasionally I blew it, or just couldn't help myself, and had a dramatic meltdown, but these instances did not change their recovery trajectory.

One of the most critical parenting decisions I made was to seek therapy for myself. Patty is my therapist. Seeing Patty meant that one hour every week, I talked to someone who was insightful, asked the right questions, and helped me put voice to my fears and identify what was right for me and for my girls. She was a person who wouldn't tire of hearing my same worries. Much of the therapy process was comforting and validating, but there were aspects that were very hard work. These were important too. I now see Patty every three weeks. The issues have changed. I'm not sure whether the pain has lessened or my coping has just improved.

Shared Responses

When you have same gender children, close in age, there is a tendency to treat them as a cohort. Ericka, Tatum, and Emma have always been "the girls." However, they are individuals with unique personalities, and their recovery journey and grief responses were different. Birth order also contributed to a distinct trajectory. I had to remind myself that what was helpful for one daughter was not necessarily helpful for another.

There were some similarities. There was an unconscious process that occurred early on, that involved us leveraging our shared reactions to secure and define our new family. One of the similarities was a mutual sense of humor that sparked in all of them, and I believe me, from the beginning. The girls have wicked funny bones, so there was a natural tendency to gravitate toward the humorous. We even engaged in black humor. Yes, sarcastic suicide comments could produce giggles—mind you, only if we made them. During one of our mother-daughter spa outings, I remember commenting that "Daddy might not approve of the upsurge in our self-care behavior," and Ericka responded with a wry, "Well, he's not here to weigh in, is he?" We knew that *he* would've laughed and chided his womenfolk right back; our jokes and silliness were an indication that we were still us. Olof was fun-loving, and his trademark banter made our house warm and light. This set us up to have fun together even in the midst of our independent grief.

Another shared trait was the joy of storytelling. Like most families, we have a collection of tales that form our history. Our stories are now even more important, as they cement our past and ground us in our family of origin. Olof left us with many stories. A great source were stories from his father-daughter excursions. He took each of the girls on a solo adventure during their fourteenth year that included a mix of culture and outdoors adventure. In all three cases, the adventures produced stories.

     McKay Moore Sohlberg

He and Ericka climbed Mount Hood, which entailed taking their skis part way up and leaving them for the trip back down. It is a rather grueling climb for adults, let alone a fourteen-year-old. Ericka minces no words in describing the desperation her young self felt on the way back down as her body told her that it was more than done with the project. She also described the exhilaration produced when one pushes oneself and triumphs. The pain was forgotten when Daddy booked a fancy hotel room in nearby Portland, where they saw a show and had a room with a view of the peak they had just successfully climbed.

I also like to tell the story of Emma's adventure. I especially like to poke fun at Olof as I recount how he gave me a furtive call during their adventure to confess that his fourteen-year-old girl was more hearty than her Daddy, and he was a wee bit frightened. He had signed them up for kayaking lessons on the Rogue River during the day and bought play tickets to watch shows at the Oregon Shakespeare Festival in nearby Ashland during the evening. My Eagle Scout, Outdoorsman Extraordinaire, called me on his cell phone from the bank of the river during their kayak class to say that Emma was taking to the sport with gusto and was learning the rolling technique, but he was having to muster up all his courage to practice the roll and keep the faith that the guide would intercede in time to perform the rescue maneuver when he was hanging upside down underwater. I like to describe how he laughed at himself and just decided to channel Emma for the resolve to follow the guide's instruction and learn the sport.

His adventure with Tatum also ended up requiring him to rely on his daughter for courage to persist. He planned a cycling trip on their tandem bike from our house in

Eugene to Crater Lake, which is over one hundred miles and involves climbing a mountain pass. When he got home, he confessed that he had miscalculated their water needs and told of the joint grit as they ran out of water and had to press on. He laughed and said that Tatum really powered them over the pass. They were rewarded by making it on time for the famous fisherman's dinner at Steamboat Inn along the Umpqua River and had secured a story of adventure and fun.

Our oral histories not only allow us to celebrate what we had, they ground us as we move forward.

One of the similarities between the three girls that surprised me, and took some adjusting on my part, was their sense of wanting life events to continue as originally planned. In retrospect, this makes sense, but at the time, I was surprised that they wanted to get back on the proverbial horse and keep the spring agenda moving forward with little outward alteration. I had expected that they would check out, need time, and not be able to continue on as scheduled. It was heartening, and rather astonishing, that they stayed the course. While I was relieved and impressed at their resilience, it forced me to mobilize my own stamina to actualize their expectations. Very quickly, Emma had prom, AP and IB exams, senior piano recital, and graduation parties. Between Olof's death and his memorial service two weeks later, Tatum returned to Stanford and took her midterms for a very rigorous set of premed classes. Ericka moved forward full steam ahead with her Stanford graduation plans and readying her transition to medical school. They not only showed up for every event, they did so with anticipation and expectancy that the occasion would unfold as it should.

     McKay Moore Sohlberg

I believe that keeping some sense of normalcy during a time of chaos was critical to their carrying on. Instinctually, they seemed to know this, and my job was to help the events happen. They taught me another principle in parenting the newly bereaved adolescent or young adult—listen to them, and they will usually show you what they need.

Yet another similarity I observed between the girls was the comfort they received from peers. Their friends helped them heal. I remain to this day humbled by the young people in their lives. Without fail, their closest friends of such tender age and experience did not shirk from the horror of suicide, and instead embraced their new normal. During that spring and summer, our house was full of young people. Their youthful vibrancy was a salve for me. Without trying, their very presence seemed to say, "We are still here, and let's make the best of it."

Because Emma was still in high school, her friends were the most present. Claire, Emma's very dear friend, stood constant vigil with Emma at the house. I can still see her making herself useful by answering our door as mourners came by to pay their respects. She met their adult gazes with ease, saying, "Hi, I'm Emma's friend, Claire. Come on in. They're in the kitchen." Adults sometimes had a harder time meeting my eye, and you could sense them fretting about saying the wrong thing. In my experience, adults are more likely to try to explain the suicide—we do this in part because we want to protect our own family, and focusing on an explanation that distances us from having the same vulnerability is comforting. The youth in our lives seemed equipped to accept the mystery and somehow reconcile that Olof was a great dad who they liked very much and that something very bad and weird happened, but that their friend was still their same friend. I remember when Emma's friend Paton decided she would need an extra-special prom date, given all she was going through. He communicated Emma's sad story to a well-known comedian of whom Emma was a devoted fan. This actor actually made a YouTube personal prom invite on behalf of Paton that was hilarious. The girls' friends were comfortable and open with our circumstance and even creative in their methods for helping us heal.

Ericka's and Tatum's college-aged friends came from near and far to support them. I was amazed that they dropped everything and traveled to support the girls and me. Ericka's boyfriend, Lee, who at the time of this writing is now her fiancé, walked every step with her. I remember when they were home for the service, I came into the kitchen to find Lee polishing the granite counter—Olof was known for keeping them shiny. This little act of preserving a household behavior he had observed Olof doing is a very precious memory for me. Tatum's very dear friend Annie was scheduled for a Semester at Sea study program that was leaving the day of Olof's memorial service. She called to let me know she was negotiating to have the ship delay its departure so she could come be with Tatum. I told her that the very act of trying to reschedule her trip was enough. She would be with us in spirit. Similarly, Allison flew home from across the country when she was in the middle of exams in order to be at Tatum's side and honor Olof, who had been a big part of her growing up. I witnessed so many acts of true friendship from the young people in my girls' lives.

Individual Grief Bios
Below, I offer a description of the girls' early responses and challenges, with the caveat that these are my words

     McKay Moore Sohlberg

and perceptions, not theirs. The laudatory descriptions are not just a mother's pride and adoration, but an important part of my story. Each of the girls eulogized their beloved father to an audience of over one thousand people, only two weeks after learning their beloved father had killed himself. Although to me, they are one in a zillion, they are simply children who have been well loved and showed the power of the human spirit that is inherent in us all.

Ericka

Ericka was excitedly anticipating her college graduation. She had accepted her offer of medical school, and we were beginning to think about helping her find an apartment and transition to a new city. She and Olof talked often about the direction of medicine, and he was very excited about her curriculum. Ericka was also anticipating us meeting Lee's parents. By now, she and Lee were quite serious, and graduation was going to be the meeting of the parents. When Olof died, Ericka was looking at making a life transition to commence a career that her father had inspired. But now he wouldn't be there to help her get started. He wouldn't meet her boyfriend's family. He was gone.

Ericka is the oldest of the three girls and has many qualities typical of the oldest child. She is achievement focused and conscientious. I watched her doggedly wrap up her college tenure, support Tatum as she took her exams, and begin the preparation to move. I remember when I could not figure out how to use Olof's bike rack and was struggling to pack up the car, she expressed frustration that Olof was not there to help with his duties. She expressed the feelings that sometimes the rest of us were afraid to voice, which was very helpful. *Where was he?* It was a fair question.

He was missing all her ceremonies. She received the honor of Phi Beta Kappa at Stanford a week after Olof died—an honor he too had received at Stanford, and she had to accept it in a ceremony without her father in the audience. I have a deep pain when I think of her white coat ceremony where they give the new medical students their first white coats to mark the start of their medical school education. It was a beautiful auditorium, and I was so proud of my girl. They then asked all of the physicians in the audience to stand up. There was no Olof standing up. She was part of a legacy that was invisible on that day. She approached her grief with honest pain, but somehow did not let her despair prevent her from moving forward. I am grateful that she let me into the medical arena and allowed me be a substitute. She called me when she saw her first baby delivery, and we both knew that it should've been Olof, but she described it to me in full medical terms just as she would have to him. Her tenacity has been inspirational to many.

> Eulogy excerpt from Ericka: *I'd like to share some-thing I wrote at age ten about Daddy for a fifth-grade school assignment. I titled it "Daddy through My Eyes." [She then read the child autobiography assign-ment describing Olof's marvels.] My ten-year-old self proved to be prophetic. This is who Daddy was my entire life—gentle, brilliant, loving, extraordinary— and I am still so proud.*
>
> *I also want to share one story that feels emblematic of our journey together. Daddy and I ran our third marathon together last fall. Naturally, it was the Nike women's marathon—it was him and thousands of women running across San Francisco. Of course, he*

     McKay Moore Sohlberg

Tatum

Tatum was a sophomore at Stanford, navigating an aca-
demically intense spring term as she followed her premed
curriculum. She had just begun formulating her major in
pediatric global health and was excitedly sharing her exploration of social justice and public health issues with Olof, as
these were shared interests. After Olof's death, she returned

to campus to take exams and stay the premed course. Our near nightly phone calls with shared tears were a gift to me. What was impressive was her receptivity. She was open to reassurance and sought comfort when she needed it. She found adults in her life at Stanford, including a pastor and a professor, who were present and caring. Tatum's receptivity to people when they reached out allowed her to manage her grief in order to keep on the track that she had chosen. We talked about extending her time at Stanford to allow her to take some time off, and she considered it fully. Characteristic of Tatum, she was thoughtful when presented with options, and made a choice that was best for her. She said she wanted to attempt to follow her program so she could graduate on time. She assured me that she would remain open if the plan did not work.

Very soon after Olof died, Tatum was offered a position in a cognitive psychology lab for the summer. This meant that she would not return home as planned and would be living in a new circumstance while she was still fresh with her grief. She would be separated from Ericka, Emma, and me, as we would all be at home in Eugene. Tatum expressed excitement to have received the lab position and wanted to pursue it. I worried that her not coming home meant that she was not facing her grief. I sought counsel from friends and professionals, many of whom said it would probably be best for her to come home. I told Tatum my concerns, and she agreed that they might hold some validity. Again, she wisely devised a bail-out option, and we agreed I would come visit her and check in face to face. Tatum finished out the summer position and loved the lab, but her summer was not without tremendous emotional challenges. I still have heartbreaking flashbacks when I see her picture on my cell phone and

 McKay Moore Sohlberg

remember how many times that summer I answered her call and was met with a long, silent latency as she struggled to get the words out to say how sad she felt. She navigated a seesaw with the stimulation of learning and engagement while confronting her loss. Tatum needed to know that, in spite of her grief, she could still perform and move forward. That independent summer provided her the reassurance. She not only finished Stanford on time as planned, she engaged fully in her communities and made them better places for all.

Eulogy excerpt from Tatum: *Whatever we liked, Daddy made it happen. Whether it was Emma's theater, our piano, or the countless sports we dabbled in over the years, he supported us. He sat next to us on the piano bench during a 6:00 a.m. practice every morning and drove us to the mountains every weekend to ski. He was there to help us when we needed it, but he always made it clear things were optional. We should do what we love. Daddy pushed us just the right amount.*

The summer each of us turned fourteen, Daddy took us each on a special adventure. He and Ericka climbed Mount Hood, followed by a theater night in Portland. Emma and Daddy took kayaking lessons on the Rogue and went to plays in Ashland in the evening. For my adventure, Daddy and I rode our tandem bike from our house to Crater Lake and spent the night in Steamboat Springs. He took each daughter on an individual adventure. He helped us become our own people.

I remember a couple of years ago when Daddy and I ran the Eugene half-marathon together. We hadn't really trained, and by mile twelve, I was really hurting. Daddy squeezed my hand to give me a surge of energy, but I held on. I remember saying, "Daddy, don't let go, or I won't finish." We both knew that I was making it more difficult. Holding hands is not really conducive to running, particularly when one person is literally hanging on the other. But he just held tighter. He got me through the finish line.

Just a couple of days ago, as I was falling asleep, still in that phase between sleep and wake, I had a dream. It wasn't a dream where I could distinguish people or faces. In this dream, all I knew was that I was sad. Then I felt the unmistakable feeling of a strong, almost too-firm grip. Daddy was holding my hand.

Emma

Emma was seventeen years old and in the throes of a busy senior spring. She had decided to attend the University of Michigan musical theatre program. A great comfort is that her daddy knew that she had been accepted into this prestigious arts program, a dream that Emma had held for many years. At the time of his death, she was two days out from opening night of her school play, *Noises Off*, where she had a lead role. *Noises Off* is a hilarious comedy, a farce to beat all farces, that requires that actors have impeccable, slapstick timing. A difficult genre for an actor grappling with a sudden loss. Emma's school drama program was somewhat renowned in our state, and these young actors had worked hard and had this complex play completely wired. Without Emma's role, the play could not open. She thought about it for a day, and then texted her director and said, "Tell the cast I will be at dress rehearsal tomorrow. It's what my dad would've wanted." That is Emma. The play ran for six shows during the initial weeks after Olof died. She was in character, hilarious, and the play was marvelous. I learned a lot about my child watching her from the back of the dark theater. She did the play for her fellow cast members, for her father, but mostly for herself. She knew what she needed, and she had the strength to do it. That is how she's navigated her grief.

An early image of Emma is emblazoned in my mind that captures my perception of her grief process. She was in the midst of high stakes exams for advanced placement and her international baccalaureate diploma. She had decided to take the exams as scheduled and continued to prepare for them. One morning, I came downstairs to wish her luck on a test and found her sitting at the kitchen table staring into space. There were rivers of silent tears running down her face. She was crying without making a single sound. She looked me directly in the eye, allowing me to see the depth of her pain, picked up her backpack, adjusted it properly on her shoulder, gave a slight reassuring nod to let me know she would be okay, and walked resolutely out the front door. There was something raw and powerful about the soundless weeping for her father in the context of going to school like a regular high school kid. She allowed herself to feel her deep internal wounds, but the pain was hers alone, and I knew that there was nothing I could do to lessen it. I also knew she would figure it out.

Eulogy from Emma: *Daddy was hilarious. He had a nickname for everyone and everything. You all probably were not called by your name in the Sohlberg household, even if you didn't know it. Growing up, we thought Starbucks was named Starbuckles 'cause that's what Daddy called it. And that the Café Espresso Roma coffee shop was actually named Daddy's Favorite Muffin Store. Kinkos was stinkos. Tatum was T-bone. Ericka was E, and I was the Mooz.*

If we wanted a piggyback ride, we had to wait on the third stair. This was called the "third stair rule." We had piggyback rides long after most kids had grown out of it.

If there was dancing at a party, he danced. We recently went to the Marashis' Persian New Year party, and he jumped right in—he actually wasn't a very good dancer but didn't care. Some of you will recognize the signature Olof move. It's all in the shoulders.

Whatever music we were into, he got into. During my middle school Kelly Clarkson phase, Daddy was frequently heard throughout the house belting "Since U Been Gone." Daddy took us to the Dixie Chicks concert and was the solo parent who excitedly took seven girls to the John Mayer concert. He shared it all.

Daddy could be serious too. I could tell him anything. It was a hard spring in Eugene, and he processed it with me.

I am who I am because he shared in my passions, passed on his, and loved me like no daughter has ever been loved.

The girls each are traveling their own journey laden with its own challenges and triumphs. As a parent, there have been many judgment calls, and I've tried to tiptoe out into

     McKay Moore Sohlberg

the recovery landscape, test the waters, and then do what seems best at that time. Sometimes I'm spot on, and sometimes I land a bit left of center. I do think that refusing to live under the shroud of suicide and being willing to shout our pride in our family life has helped.

Tomorrow marks the fourth Mother's Day of me flying solo as a parent. For the first time, I will be alone, without any of the girls, but it's okay. Actually, it's better than okay—it is great. The reason that I will be alone is because they transcended tragedy and are fully embracing what this life has to offer them. Ericka is with her fiancé, Lee, helping him prepare for his qualifying doctorate exams. On her finger is the wedding ring that Olof had made for me, that contains the wedding diamonds of his paternal grandmother and my maternal grandmother. She and Lee asked to have that ring, with no alterations. They will add their own blissful marital years to the one hundred collective years of marriage that those stones have symbolized. A wonderful cycle. Tatum is in California working for a family health clinic and preparing to move back to Oregon to start medical school. She is working to increase healthcare access for underserved populations, continuing a cause that was deep for her father. Emma is in Senegal, where she has been studying abroad for almost five months, living with a local family, studying Islamic culture, playing the kora, and learning the local tongue, Wolof. Global citizenship was another characteristic that Olof worked to instill in the children. Tomorrow, I will celebrate their resilience. While their healing continues, and I know they have forever pain, they appear to be building on the foundation their father established, rather than getting stuck in his illness. For this I am truly grateful.

Everyone's journey, prior circumstances, children, and selves are different. Navigation of tragedy is deeply personal and there is no right way. I know this. We are just one family. When asked, my advice to others has been to listen to stories and advice of those who have been there, and pick out only that which makes sense for you. And then poke a little fun at the rest. Have at it with our stories. The girls and I would laugh with you.

 McKay Moore Sohlberg

CHAPTER SEVEN

Are You There God? It's Me, McKay

During the first two years after Olof's death, I had flashbacks of scenes from a tweenie book my friends and I devoured in middle school. Judy Blume's 1970 novel *Are You There God? It's Me Margaret* chronicled the challenges of an angsty prepubescent girl wrestling with buying her first bra, getting her period, and liking boys. The main conflict in the story, though, comes from Margaret's quest to sort out matters of religion, as her mother is Christian and her father is Jewish, and she feels mixed up. As she tries to deal with her confusion over religion and puberty, she frequently summons help by saying, "Are you there God? It's me, Margaret." At fifty-one years of age, I related to Margaret. I experienced identity issues and angst amidst a need for a spiritual compass to guide me through my confusion and pain. More than once, I heard myself say out loud, "Are you there God? It's me, McKay," followed by a desperate presentation of a dilemma or fear. In my adult life, I have not been prone to uttering prayers outside the familiar, prescribed prayers in Sunday church services. I can, however, remember as a preteen initiating some chats, and a bit of bargaining, with God before maturity seemed to spoil this resource. After Olof died, I seemed to involuntarily regress (progress?) to using Margaret and my young self's help-seeking tactic and uttered an occasional, "Excuse me, I need some help here." The interesting phenomenon is that I often felt better.

Some background. I am a bit of a spiritual dabbler. While I enjoy contemplating the profound and admire that wise, transcendent nature that I perceive many of those who are strong in their religions and philosophies hold, I have never personally been able to devote myself to matters of the spirit. At the end of the day, I am a scientist. An extremely rational, practical, fairly skeptical, critical academic. It's not all bad, except for when you find yourself at a life crossroad that reason and logic can't help. Death, particularly suicide, leaves survivors riddled with unanswerable questions, desperate for explanations that will never be found. I so badly wanted to be comforted by the loving beliefs of well wishers. I wish I could've been helped by the permutations of the common themes: "He is at peace now"; "He's in a better place"; "He's with the angels"; or "God has a plan." I also wish I could've been more receptive and experienced the comfort others reported when they deeply felt his presence in a cloud formation, a gust of wind, or a bird hopping at their feet. I was jealous of my friends who would text me a picture of a full and vibrant rainbow and describe how they could feel him. But these messenger gifts did not come to me. I just felt Olof's searing absence.

     McKay Moore Sohlberg

I simply don't believe that people stay intact with awareness of their earthly selves as they ascend to some heavenly destination with only the godly components of their souls carrying forward. I wish I did. I also don't think that God planned for Olof to die violently and leave the girls and me with such confusion and for him to miss out on the joys and fruits of a life that he'd so lovingly and enthusiastically constructed. I was left with an inability to be comforted by the belief offerings of others that seemed so fundamental to their own healing.

Me: *Are you there God? It's me, McKay. I need some spiritual comfort here. You see, I just don't think people go to Heaven when they die. I definitely don't think this was part of any plan. I'm not sure I see a role for religion in my life right now, but I feel constrained by my rational self. Thoughts? Hello? Are you there God? It's me, McKay.*

Faint Response: *Well, you say a lot about what you DON'T believe, any thoughts on what you DO believe?*

My effort to transcend the limits of reason and logic led me back to church. I had taken a break after Olof died, as it was just too sad to sit alone in the family pew where we had worshipped for over twenty years. I realized that church for me was largely about enjoying the warmth and security of singing familiar hymns, being deepened by the beautiful poetry of the prayers, and feeling connected as our family sat together among a community of people who tried to make the world a better place. Suddenly, none of that offered the same comfort or importance. Now, I was looking to church to help me manage the ravages of a situation that challenged many of my previous beliefs. The good news is that I was raised in a church, the Episcopal Church, that likes skeptics and scientists, invites questioning, and even celebrates the capacity to reason. I could bring all the hard questions and my "I simply don't believe that" and still feel welcomed.

My church also likes ritual, which helped me get out of my head and start just being. The bells and whistles, as Olof called them—the robes, procession, organ, and occasional incense—helped me transcend. The Episcopal Church is sort of an all-comers' operation for people who kind of like things a bit fancy. The fact that you can sit in your pew with a person on your left who is a biblical literalist and a person on your right who views the stories of the Great Book as largely beautiful myths and metaphor, and they both gather communally around the same table, greatly appeals to me. I'm grateful I had a context from which to wrestle with glaring spiritual needs that life's grisly turn had thrust upon me.

So what do I believe? My anxious contemplations in the sleepless nights, early morning running talks with my friends, writings by authors such as Marcus Borg, John Spong, and Anne Lamott all provided accessible and inclusive spiritual nuggets. For me to heal, I had to wrestle with the big questions around death. It did not work for me to ignore the nagging call to think about God. Nor did it work to relegate Olof to just being gone, end of story. I think one of God's greatest gifts is our mind, a mind that is programmed to contemplate the big questions if we get out of the way and let it. My circumstances created a need to question and reflect, and somewhere along the way, I began to formulate the beginnings of my own spiritual creed. With tremendous humility at its crude simplicity, at the time of this writing, I have four budding religious convictions. The good news is that it is a work in progress.

     McKay Moore Sohlberg

I believe that God is Love, a powerful force.

By Love, I don't mean the starry-eyed, warm and fuzzy emotion. I believe Love is an actual unexplainable force, not a feeling. God is the force that connects us to the people in our daily lives, to family members and friends in distant places, to those who have died but occupy a very real place in our beings. Love prompts us to act on behalf of not only those close to us, but people we may not know at all but whom we know need our help. Love is the force that moves us to be the very best that we can be. It is this capacity to engage in the force of Love that makes us unique as human beings. *(Adapted from a Sunday sermon by my friend and church liturgist Sharon Rodgers.)*

This first belief in my credo is the easiest for me. It is when I open myself to Love, both in giving and receiving, that God becomes clear to me. Love has been my salvation for recovery from Olof's death.

I believe that faith is largely about trust and
actively working to feel God's presence.

Faith seems like an essential component of any type of spiritual conviction and is a real bugaboo when you are wrestling with the "whys" of suicide. I resonate with Marcus Borg's teaching of faith. He rejects the modern "distortion of faith" with its definitive "truths" and reminds us what this type of faith would've looked like before the Enlightenment. Instead, he examines the ancient ways of defining *faith* by exploring its Hebrew and Latin roots and offers several different definitions. To give clarity, for each definition, he provides the opposite meaning. Two definitions work for me, so I'm adopting them into my credo. First, *faith is trust.* The opposite of trust, or truth, is actually *not* doubt but the self-preoccupying force of anxiety. If you have faith, you are not anxious. I have a long way to go in this department, but I believe that faith can help me get there. When I work to actively trust in myself and those around me, the dark times laden with anxiety do lighten. Secondly, I believe faith is about *fidelity to a relationship,* in this case with God (or Love). The opposite, of course, is infidelity or separation from God. I think I fluctuate on this dimension. Sometimes I feel loyal and singular in my connection to God, but it's often fleeting and dependent upon external events in my life going well, so I'm a bit of a fickle follower. I see that the trust and fidelity are intertwined and often require me to actively seek a deliberate state of mind. My faith is evolving, however. Coping with Olof's death has pushed the envelope and forced me to examine my faith and, in so doing, is steadily bringing me a sense of grounding.

---

*I think that when people die, their spirit lives
on in the people they have touched, who in turn
will live on in the people they touch, and so on.
This is the resurrection.*

I cannot say what I "believe" happens after people die because no one actually "knows." Stating a *belief* does not solve *unknowing.* Instead, I find myself grateful for the power to imagine, observe, and explore my inner thoughts, which are unique gifts of our species. I've been forced to

     McKay Moore Sohlberg

engage these gifts in an attempt to understand a world where Olof no longer occupies a physical presence. I see how his presence lives on in me and the girls and in our friends and family and the hundreds of patients he touched. I see how his life and his death have shaped individuals and communities. I think this might be the crux of spirituality, a condition that provides eternal life, a human resurrection.

About five months after Olof died, I took a pilgrimage to France to complete part of a trip we had planned. I went running in the early morning along the old stone seawalls above a very rough and cold Brittany sea. Mind you, I do not like being cold. In fact, I detest it. Olof, on the other hand, would jump in glacier water and swim in every river, ocean, or lake that revealed itself. (The girls have inherited this hearty trait.) As I ran along, I felt this strong compulsion to go swimming in the ocean. Did I mention it was rainy and cold? I found myself taking off my running shoes, descending the wall, jogging down to the sand, plunging into the ocean and submerging myself as if conducting my own baptism. It felt wonderfully exhilarating. I paddled around close to the shore before I emerged to retrieve my running shoes and returned dripping wet with seawater to the hotel lobby. Over the years, I had sat gingerly at the edge of many frigid bodies of water and watched Olof enjoy the refreshing shock. Something about him being gone compelled me to do something counter to my nature and wholly part of him. Through his death I was changed—what had been aversive was pleasurable. I think we are connected through death and beyond death. Sometimes the connection is physical with shared DNA;

sometimes it is emotional, forged by continuous time and shared experience or even from a single influential interaction. Sometimes we are connected with a person who died that we never even met because their stories affect us. I think the God within people lives on in many ways and is continually resurrected.

I am comforted by thinking about the connectedness of the departed with the living. I like to imagine eternal cycles replete with the myriad emotions we humans are privileged to possess—joy, sadness, anger, reconciliation, learning, despair, love—occurring iteratively through the generations.

I believe random bad things happen.

Sometimes people get dealt a bad card—like depression. This randomness is part of the universal condition. We need dark to see light; we need randomness to have wonder.

Almost three years of questioning have led me to these four simple thoughts on spirituality. A modest treatise, I know, but given the circumstances, it's progress.

Prayer and Signs: A Reluctant Evolution

As I confessed, my conversations with God have been fairly limited and undeveloped. They likely would have been permanently relegated to the occasional pleading in a perceived crisis and uttering the Sunday Standards had I not lost Olof or experienced such trauma. I suspect that intense pain or worry is a frequent catalyst for finding the power of prayer. In my old life, I might have spurned this as needy folks looking for a crutch and wondered why they didn't employ the resources God gave them to problem solve, relinquish, and for heaven's sake, figure things out. However, I've learned that deep pain begets insight, so I view some things differently now. Mind you, it is unwanted insight; my increased understanding of humanity feels like an unwelcome booby prize. Regardless, I found myself experimenting with prayer, but it felt forced and inauthentic. My priest made me feel better when he told me that, in general, Episcopalians aren't that great at everyday prayer. It'll come, he assured me, but maybe not in the ways or places I expect.

One of the facilitators of my very nascent prayer behavior is my dear friend and running mate of fifteen years, Jani. She actually knows how to pray. For years, I was witness to her occasional conversations with God. Sometimes they were on my behalf. I'd be worried or anxious about something and she'd say, "Let's pray." This meant that she'd initiate this very natural sounding conversation asking for insight or grace or peace while expressing gratitude, and I'd listen. It was kind of like giving her my prayer proxy. It worked for me, as I didn't have to get messy with this prayer business. Then, one time she was facing a situation that was scary, so I thought I'd return the favor. I was motivated because I adore Jani and don't like it when her world is hard. I thought I did a pretty good job and felt a little better afterward. Interestingly, all of our prayers were while running in the early mornings and when crossing one of the many bridges of our Oregon rivers that are lined by running trails. We'd stop, hold hands, and look at the water rushing below us. It was as if the crossing that joined the two banks served as a metaphor for us to try to transcend our earthly worries and gain perspective.

After Olof died, we had a lot to pray about. She continued to lead the spiritual petitions on our bridges, but I began to look forward to them and think about what I wanted to say for the previous two miles leading up to the water crossing. The natural wonders on our Oregon trails supported my budding transcendence. I had always loved seeing the beautiful blue heron, and our running trio—Jani, Cary, and I—would exclaim over the bird when we were graced by a sighting. It seemed like after Olof died, the herons were more plentiful. I began searching for them on every run, glancing up in the trees and along the brushy riverbanks, and they became my spirit bird. Their magnificent wingspan and enigmatic elegance along with their always solo and completely still stature fascinated me. Somehow they began symbolizing Olof's ongoing presence and the mysteries that exceed human understanding. My rational self opened up. Prayer and a spiritual sign. Who would've thought?

I knew I had evolved when I began to feel the need to bless the girls whenever they left home and were returning to school. After Olof died, I was annoyingly tearful whenever it was time for them to return to their schools or jobs. I cut myself some slack since goodbyes to ones you love are always hard, and when the departing have constituted your very reason for continuing, kissing them farewell till next time is emotional. My response, however, evolved to a deep need to bless them with a travel prayer when they left our house. My girls had been amazingly respectful of all of my memorializing, so when I announced that I now wanted to say a travel prayer every time they left Eugene, there were no objections. Okay, so there wasn't any fanfare

 McKay Moore Sohlberg

or encouragement, but sweet tolerance is appreciated. At first, I tried a prayer out of our church prayer book, but it was not quite right, so I had to write my own. Sometimes I forget to do it when they leave; then I have to say it by myself or call them on their cell phones. The prayer is in the kitchen "junk drawer," as the kitchen is often the last place we are gathering before heading out the front door. The prayer eases my pain when they leave and helps me find faith they'll return as they should. I suspect their children will be subject to this travel prayer ritual as I'm now kind of bully on it. The lesson? Prayer eases. Here's the travel prayer for those who might want to adopt it:

> *Dear God—Please watch over your child (children) as she (they) goes(go) forth. We give thanks for the time we have spent together and the love we have shared while in each other's company in this blessed home and community. Help us to feel that love while we are apart and to touch others with it as we go about our learning and work. Bless her (their) travels and bring her (them) safely back to me when it is time. Amen.*

Get Over Yourself

Earlier I lamented the necessary, but frustrating, narcissism imposed by grief. There is this seemingly compulsory seesaw where your seat is planted firmly on the ground as you wallow in the depths of profound pain until you actively push yourself upward and are able to see yourself as your own agent of choice responsible for fashioning your existence. Then, sometime later, you may plummet back to a hard landing on the ground. Wallowing is kind of the default position early on. I often image a seesaw where Olof had to bail, and it slammed me to the ground, leaving me sitting unaccompanied and unbalanced. Over time it has felt as if I spend less time on the ground. I actually schedule times when it is both convenient and therapeutic to wallow, sitting with my dead weight on the seesaw of life and let myself feel the sadness of the empty seat across from me. As the months turned into the initial years, I began to feel my existential stirrings, and my inner voice would command, "Get over yourself already." My feet would push off, and I would slowly rise and take responsibility for my world—balanced by all the wonderful relationships: past, current, and those yet to be discovered.

Sometimes it helps me to remember that I am just one of seven billion people on the planet and that the world was turning on its axis for an unfathomably long time before Olof and I got here, it continued to do so after he died, and it will continue after I am gone as well. I kind of remember feeling weirdly surprised in the beginning that the sun still rose and set when my life was in such a turmoil. At the same time, it was a comfort. Things would continue. Sure I matter, but I am part of a much bigger order in the universe. This helps me keep my troubles in perspective.

One of the activities I was forced to do early on that nudged me into remembering that my issues did not occupy everyone's center stage was traveling. I had to take a number of solo trips both for work and to visit my daughters. Traveling brings a sense of anonymity and has this way of leveling humanity's playing field. You are just a nameless passenger in airline seat number 3D, putting up your tray

    McKay Moore Sohlberg

table and seat back when commanded. You will arrive at your destination with all the other people on your plane. Nothing you can do can alter this. There is no special (yet) priority part of the airplane for those who want to pay more to arrive twenty minutes early. No one on the plane knows your life story, so there are no special breaks or treatment. I never received an extra packet of peanuts or those really good biscuits that Delta flights offer just because I looked sad. I always had to ask.

Traveling was difficult. First, I had to leave the cocoon of my house. Second, Olof had been the one to make my travel plans and figure out the flights, ground transportation, and hotels. Third, he was the one who tracked my every travel move. Now there was often no one I needed to call if my flight was late or canceled. My car would still be in the Eugene parking lot when I got there. I traveled a lot and was one of those unlucky few with bad travel karma who was often stuck in a random city overnight. There was no Olof to listen to petty whining about a rude flight attendant or my seat partner when she snored, overshared, put her feet in my space, or brought aboard a smelly tuna sandwich. On the other hand, there was something therapeutic in being a bit anonymous and wholly responsible for my travel.

A solo voyage is always somewhat of a pilgrimage and encourages reflection. I remember that once I was staying in a hotel in Cincinnati where I was consulting on a research grant. The hotel was right near the hospital where I was working, and the ambulance sirens were loud throughout the night. Sirens had been part of my PTSD profile and could put me back to the horror of running into the street toward the police to urge them to hurry and save Olof. For months afterward, a siren would time travel me to that black night and produce unwanted images and deep fear. As I lay in my hotel bed with the sirens re-traumatizing me, I remembered an "Are you there God? It's me, McKay" moment. I pleaded with God to make the sounds stop. Although the sirens continued, their effects gradually lessened. The fear and nausea receded. My brain slowly realized these sirens were for other people, and they were independent of me. There was something about being all alone, far from home in a strange context, that prompted me to ask for help and allowed me to be receptive to change. Since then, the sirens have triggered very few flashbacks.

Traveling was weirdly transcendent. It somehow reminded me that I was still among the living, and it was up to me to join with humanity and make the most of this gift of life. I began to look the hotel clerks and airline counter staff in the eye and give my thank-yous more freely. I was more aware of people around me and felt oddly connected with them. On a more trifling note, traveling helped me feel more connected when I had to figure out travel arrangements and problem solve. I reclaimed a sense of self. Amidst the scary and the sad, traveling was helpful in reminding me that sometimes I need to get over myself and join my brothers and sisters on the airport escalators leading to the next terminal and figure out my flight arrangements.

Olof's death has and continues to change me. It has forced me to wrestle with matters of the spirit. I have a rudimentary personal creed with some fledgling beliefs and thoughts. I now sometimes write and say prayers and they help me. I have a glimmer of an understanding that the

 McKay Moore Sohlberg

mysterious universe is very big, and I am just a tiny, albeit important, speck along with all the other important specks, on one of its beautiful planets. It appears to me that the Master Designer of this universe is a loving, powerful force that somehow fashioned a paradox with two contrasting truths—nothing lasts forever and everything lasts forever.

CHAPTER EIGHT

Never Say Never

Would I ever feel truly happy again? This was a secret question that gnawed deep within me for a long time. From the beginning, even during times of despair, I was able to feel intense gratitude and love, especially for my children. But I wondered whether I'd ever feel a personal happiness beyond the gratitude. I had always said that if something happened to Olof, I would *never* marry again. I would have had everything one could wish for. Besides, I'd never really dated, and it did not look fun.

My naive, uninformed self did not anticipate some of the emotions that come with being widowed. In the safe, confidential sanctity of my therapy sessions, I lamented my loss of womanhood. I told Patty that I worried I'd become a shriveled old woman. I cried with self-pity over the fact that Olof was no longer there to gently brush my hair out of my face, bring me coffee and flowers, surprise me with romantic getaways, and make me feel sexy. I confessed that I liked feeling adored by my beautiful husband. Then I'd be riddled with guilt about my superficial vanity, as these losses were nothing compared to the important stuff. I think loss of romance and amour that is shared between spouses is another one of those death subjects that our culture relegates to the taboo. It's OK to talk about loss of companionship, the burden of extra tasks, and the pain of parenting solo, but not so OK to detail the loss of intimacy that can only be shared with that one person. So, it stayed between my therapist and me. I missed Olof in a zillion ways, but holding hands, pillow talk, and sharing morning coffee were way up there.

Very quickly, people began to talk, or at least hint, about the possibility of my finding love again. They did this by telling me stories of their cousins or friends who met someone. Frankly, I found this repulsive. I still do. Husbands are not replaceable. It is on my list of "never say this when talking to the bereaved." As the months went on, however, I entertained private contemplations about whether I'd grow old alone, but again, this was a tight-lipped fear that was not comfortable to share. I also was not sure that the alone state might not be the preferred long-term option if I could not have Olof. I would try to imagine myself as this very cool older woman, inde-pendent, dedicated to family and community, traveling around the globe. Then I'd watch a movie, work in the garden, or take a walk alone and the glamour would fade.

I wanted to feel better about flying solo and project a chin up attitude. I think I felt like this would best honor Olof. This is slightly embarrassing, but I went through a phase of thinking that if I "practiced" and worked at it, I could become that self-actualized person who transi-tioned gracefully to single life. A peaceful, martyred wife who found comfort in her past, admired by all for how she bravely continued on alone. Too bad I wasn't born in another era or culture. I could have reveled in my black frock; even better if I lived on a cliff with a moor so I could be that tragic character with wind whipping at my black widow's garb as the sea crashed below me. I took a more practical, contemporary route, however, to mastering my new station. I instituted a ritual that I privately called "widow practice." Perhaps a bit odd, but my coping strategy often involved setting a goal and working at it. I decided that at least a couple of times a week, I would forgo the kind offers of dinner with friends, stay home, and resist eating standing up while staring into the open fridge. I would practice making a real meal for one person with leftovers for my lunch. Widow practice had set criteria: place mat, cloth napkin, and at least one item that I cooked. I could have one glass of wine, but not two. I was not allowed to use the phone during my meal, and was required to be my own company. (This particular rule didn't last very long; I loosened my guidelines to allow reading while eating.) This went on for about a month, and then I told Patty about my self-tutelage, and she suggested I at least consider changing the name. This led me to drop the whole structure. Some things you just can't practice.

Art has been my hairdresser for many years. We have interesting conversations about our life philosophies. One conversation stuck with me. As he worked on giving me some nice highlights, he told me that he thinks some people are just "couples' people." They are programmed to be part of a twosome—sort of like being an extrovert or an intro-vert; people either operate more fully in solo or in tandem. I don't know whether I was innately programmed that way, but at the very least, I was fully conditioned and imprinted

    McKay Moore Sohlberg

as being part of a pair. I completely relate to mallard ducks that mate for life. I loved the interdependence Olof and I shared. Neither one of us was very big on independent getaways—he did not do guy outings, and I did not plan girlfriend getaways. The imprinting and mating for life is awesome…unless that person dies. Then you are left with being a couples' person but unable to fathom having that with anyone other than your mate.

My peculiar, private musings about my new identify as a woman morphed over the months. I remember a stage where I thought that in order for me to really allow someone into my life, he would have to meet a challenging laundry list of demands.

For starters:
He would have to have known Olof.
He would have to have really admired Olof.
He would have to have experienced substantial trauma and preferably death.
He would have to be in counseling to cope with his trauma.
He would have to believe that my girls were amazing.
He would have to accept and even urge me to prioritize my daughters.
He would have to support and encourage my budding, albeit somewhat fragile, independence.
He would have to not weary of my tears.
He would have to be comfortable sharing his own tears.
He would have to have good chemistry with all of my extended family, no exceptions.
He would have to be smart.

He would have to offer insightful comments when I was angsty.

He would have be engaged in his community.
He would have to be a Democrat.
He would have to be an Episcopalian.
He would have to be funny.
He would have to laugh at my jokes.
He would have to be an outdoorsperson.
He would have to like to weed in the garden.
He would have to be physically fit.

There was more. It doesn't take a psychologist to read between the lines: the list was a deal-breaker. The lengthy and specific combination of factors made this list impossible to grant. Hence, I was saved from having to deal with the issue at all. No one could meet these criteria, so I could get on with the job of accepting my new situation and work to embrace the new normal.

In retrospect, I wonder if I had unconsciously devised that list to fit Greg, who had been hanging around and making himself very useful. Our friendship had an indefinable, limbo quality that was not easily classified by us, let alone others. Olof and I had been friends with Greg and Kathy. Not inner circle friends, but definitely the go-out-to-dinner-the-four-of-us-every-now-and-again type of friends. Our kids had been in the same school program since kindergarten. Greg had cycled and skied on occasion with Olof. Kathy and I had been on school committees together and enjoyed each other's company and occasionally emailed funny musings about our children. We went out to lunch together a few times. When Kathy was diagnosed with ovarian cancer, Olof and I were part of their family's

     McKay Moore Sohlberg

support circle. Olof had treated Kathy briefly during her cancer course. The story is more complicated than Greg losing Kathy to cancer. She battled her disease to stay alive to see their son graduate from high school. She made it, but their son did not. Greg's story is his, but in a tragic nutshell, he and Kathy lost their cherished eighteen-year-old boy, their only child together, to a freak accident just five months before Kathy succumbed to her disease. Olof died in between these two horrible events. Greg and I had a lot to talk about over coffee. Grief buddies, an acquaintance neither of us wanted, but both of us appreciated. Misery loves company, and we had despair to share.

While it is tempting to end the Greg story here, and say that our relationship gradually evolved from trauma pals, to friends, to confidantes, with a final culmination as romantic partners, that version would be a lie. I will resist the strong pull of revisionist history to finesse the story and write how I found a second beautiful love and peacefully embraced it. Honesty compels me to admit that opening myself to love again was complicated. I doubt this is unique to suicide survivors.

It is quite scary to "love again." So I hung out at the "like again" stage for a long while, not yet ready to explore possibilities. That worked for me. I had a lot to wrestle with. Guilt featured as a prominent barrier to allowing myself to explore all new relationships, including romance.

I was plagued by guilt. All flavors of guilt. Survivor's guilt was at the top of the list. Olof's disease robbed him of everything that he held dear. If he couldn't live out our couples' happiness, then it didn't seem right for me to fill my empty heart, or even to pursue fun (unless it was connected to moving the girls forward). I remember the second Thanksgiving without him. Emma, Tatum, and Olof's sister, Kristen, and I decided we would abandon the turkey feast tradition and spend the holiday on a New York extravaganza. We stayed in a fancy hotel in the Upper East Side in Manhattan, and took advantage of the elegant spa treatments, doormen, and plush living quarters. We walked from our hotel across Central Park to find the perfect place to watch the Macy's parade, saw three excellent plays, ate at wonderful restaurants, and made memories that we still relish. I found myself pursuing fun *just for the sake of enjoyment*. Periodically during the three days, a nagging feeling crept into my consciousness from the deep recesses of my mind. It was kind of like that feeling you have when you know you are forgetting something, but you don't know what it is, so you stop and try to remember. When I stopped to ponder, I recognized the unwelcome sensation of guilt. I was having fun, and he couldn't share it. Minus the spa, he would have embraced every activity with gusto. It wasn't fair. It wasn't right. How could I have fun when he couldn't?

I also had parent guilt. My children would never have a father again. It felt like that space should remain a sacred placeholder. I should stand tall and strong and be their mother and their father, avoiding any actions that would complicate their lives. The "should" was firm and loud and clear. When Greg came by for a visit, and the girls were home, it just seemed wrong. He would show interest and enthusiasm, and the girls would feel their boundaries being violated, and frankly, so did it I. He'd bring by a favorite food, fix a broken item, and receive tempered appreciation. He felt our family cohesion, and with his wife and son gone,

     McKay Moore Sohlberg

it was a salve to him. Truth be told, he did not read the room well. His enthusiasm and overly loose boundaries due to his own losses and needs did not engender trust. The girls were kind and polite, but not encouraging. Rationally, I knew that this sentiment was the most healthy and appropriate response, but there just seemed like no easy way forward. I was falling further "in like" with Greg. We enjoyed cycling, running, hiking, talking about politics, and eating out. He taught me some cycling skills, and I taught him to cook. While the girls were glad I had a companion, they (and I) needed our foursome tight and intact.

Guilt also came with the Comparison Game. New love would not be possible because I had already shared the most important life events with my soul mate, and by comparison, new love would always pale. Olof and I had shared late adolescence through middle age with the establishment of our very identities, including careers, and most importantly, raising a family. Even the minutiae of unimportant daily habits were vulnerable to the Comparison Game. I found my critical brain alive with, *"That's not how Olof carved a flank steak, answered the phone, rolled up his sleeves, or made my coffee."* Then there were a whole host of actions that were quite similar between Olof and Greg and that didn't satisfy me either as my petty thoughts unleashed, *"Only Olof is allowed to support that political cause, cycle fast in the local peloton, bring me flowers, and comment on how smart the girls are."* I could feel myself on occasion blaming Greg for not being Olof, and he was completely unaware of the origin of my snarky tone.

It felt like I was in a play and a few of the actors got mixed up. *"Excuse me, Greg, I think you are supposed to be on the stage across the way. Olof is actually in that role.*" One evening about a year after Olof had died, we were cooking dinner in my kitchen, cutting up veggies side by side for a stir-fry. I looked up, and there was Greg innocently chopping bok choy on the circular raised chopping block I'd given Olof, using a very dull knife because I wasn't sure how to sharpen it since Olof took care of that task. I actually said out loud, "How did *you* come to be standing here?" He knew exactly what I meant and responded, "Good question. Where's the door?" (Remember that item #16 on the list was the requirement to be funny.) But he followed it up with, "I'd actually like to stay for dinner, as it looks tasty and I'm hungry. May I?"

It took a lot of time for me to let my guard down, and getting to know each other was both a sweet and arduous process. I was not an easy companion by any stretch of the imagination, but Greg seemed to see potential. Occasionally, I would joke with him in an attempt to temper my mood swings and overall darkness: "You only have to spend a small portion of the week with me, but I'm stuck with myself 24-7." But the chemistry and friendship warranted attention. We developed our own language around the process of timidly opening ourselves up to possibilities. The phrase, "that's a *confusion*" connoted an event or characteristic that was reminiscent of his late wife, Kathy, or of Olof. It was used when one of us did something in the same rhythm or manner from our previous life. Sometimes it felt nice and sometimes not. What helped was that we were always honest and clear.

We had very different issues and backgrounds, in spite of sharing recent trauma. Greg had taken care of Kathy for four years while she was ill. He was known in our circle for being an amazing support. They had a bucket list, and he

 McKay Moore Sohlberg

made sure it was actualized. He described what it felt like to have time to say goodbye. Kathy had blessed him moving forward and encouraged him to find love again. He'd even found a note with her top choices for women to call if she needed help at the end, and I was on that list. Greg had weathered a difficult divorce by his parents and abandonment by his mother. He'd entered early relationships to fill his void, and while they did not last, one result was two children who helped to ground him and shared the pain of losing their stepmother and brother. Hence, Greg was not a stranger to resilience and picking up the pieces. In contrast, the suddenness of losing Olof, combined with my own lack of experience with adversity, made me a much slower study.

You learn a lot about a person when you share life altering tragedies. You learn whether one or both of you are consumed with your own heartbreak to the exclusion of others. You learn about how you each manage stress and view misfortune, and you get to see who they use as their go-to people for comfort. You see whether that person can comfort you, give you space, honor your situation, and be authentic. You learn whether they can both wallow and buck up and do so at the right times. I'm guessing that shared trauma is better than any electronic couples' matching algorithms for ferreting out compatible characteristics. I wouldn't recommend it as a dating strategy, however.

But since we didn't get to choose, we used our commonalities to comfort and our differences to grow.

Our growing partnership was tricky. Beyond the guilt and the Comparison Game, I worried that I was not sufficiently psychologically stable. I worried the relationship was a reaction to being lonely and bereft and therefore not the real deal. I worried that I was too broken to ever be a healthy partner. I wasn't sure I wanted to take the risk. I did not want my children to have to deal with a new and complicated situation when they had been through so much. Basically I had a host of ifs, ands, and buts. Greg was patient and unafraid of my hesitancy. He was comfortable moving forward, if a bit hasty and optimistic in his belief that our relationship was the sure route to happiness. My need for what, at times, was brutal honestly was met with return honesty and gentle acceptance.

Greg wanted to move forward in our relationship and quickly talked about marriage. I waited to "feel better." I waited to not have crying episodes and to feel like my old self. It didn't happen. Year three of Olof's death anniversary date felt as painful, if not more so, than year two. That day, I went on a solo bird-watching outing at Finley preserve, a wildlife sanctuary that Olof and I had discovered together. I watched a spotted towhee and cried hard as I remembered that the first time that I had seen that bird was at that very spot with Olof. We'd randomly brought along a bird book and excitedly identified it as we tromped through the preserve. I practiced the exercise that Patty had taught me when the pain grips you—you first localize it and examine it. It was a tightening in my throat and a painful hardness deep in my belly. As I recognized the pain and slowly breathed, it receded. I started feeling peaceful about my memories. I called my girls as I strolled about in the rain and had nice talks with each of them. I realized that I was also missing Greg and looked forward to returning to town to see him. That felt OK too. The pain and the hope could be compatible.

Slowly, I began to have some helpful insights. One critical revelation was that I was not going to get *all* better, that I would probably be crying, at least occasionally, for a

     McKay Moore Sohlberg

long long time—maybe forever. Such was the circumstance given Olof's and my relationship, our growing up together, and the deep interdependence. Such is the circumstance produced by suicide. I realized that I was continuing to heal in part through being in a relationship with Greg. I recognized that he embraced the broken *and* the whole within me. I opened myself up to receive and give love.

Occasionally, I could logically reason that my guilt was misplaced. If I denied myself the happiness of partnership, it would actually dishonor Olof. The reason I could heal in a relationship and feel the pull of love was, in part, because of him. He had loved me completely, and I was primed, if the right person came along. I also saw that my girls were moving forward in their ambitions and in their own relationships. We all knew they would forever mourn the loss of their father, and I would forever mourn the loss of the chance to grow old with him. He was gone, but the four of us were still very much alive. And he would remain alive in us. The courage to open ourselves up to what this life had to offer us was grounded in our life with Olof. I appreciated these reassuring thoughts when I was able to conjure them up, even though they were often fleeting and followed by the complicated ones shrouded with guilt and sadness.

I felt myself ever so slowly become more open to the mystery, and at times, I was partially successful in getting out of my analytical head and embracing the questions instead of trying to answer them. I got better at not comparing the empty nest scenario with the full nest that I knew with Olof. I started to feel committed to Greg and my partnership.

Bottom line: Loving again is a complicated process.

The sanctity of marriage, for me, is holy and precious. As time went forward, I became sure. I wanted to live in the state of matrimony, and I wanted to do that with Greg. This did not mean that the difficult stuff did not creep up and that we did not have to work hard to try to build a healthy partnership. But I knew this was the path I wanted. Greg and I were married in a small Episcopal church in Portland, Oregon. We exchanged vows that acknowledged our commitment to honoring the people we had loved and keeping their memories close and a part of our own union.

While our grief and loss complicated some aspects of our union, it enhanced others. Shared family time with Ericka and Lee; Tatum and Jared; Emma, and later, Taylor was a centerpiece in our union. Greg seemed to revel in joining our family, and the gradual transition to being a stepfather fulfilled him. We were happy companions deriving much enjoyment cycling in the Eugene countryside, running along the Willamette River, cooking in our kitchen, and beautifying the garden. We took a number of epic vacations that included Croatia, Patagonia, Colombia, and France. We completed several major remodels to expand the Sohlberg family home to include Greg in its house story. Both of us continued to enjoy and work hard at careers we found fulfilling. Life moved forward.

The edges on the pain and loss softened. The scar on my emotional wounds toughened. I felt Olof blessing my life or maybe relinquishing my grieving self so I could bless my own life. It was like he was giving me a small, almost imperceptible nod with a peaceful look that affirmed my new phase. I felt whole. It felt possible to integrate the past, present, and future.

Much happened during our early years of marriage. There were the stresses of me being the primary caretaker

 McKay Moore Sohlberg

for two ailing parents and subsequently grieving the death of my mom. There were also many joyous events that helped solidify us as a family. Ericka's and Tatum's jubilant weddings and Emma's successful move to New York to launch her acting career were epic highlights. Greg's children also married and began families, which gave us a chance to appreciate the preciousness of new life and to connect more deeply with his children.

Sharing the everyday was perhaps what I most cherished. I loved the tenderness and everyday ritual of Greg making me my morning coffee and delivering it to me in our bedroom. He appreciated me listening to his work stories at the end of the day, as he liked to unload and process his office day. We enjoyed Saturday "urban walks" around the neighborhood, watching a serial show on TV, and spending time in community with friends and family. I believed that our love was evolving and our previous losses would provide a foundation for a shared goal to gratefully and contentedly grow old together.

When I started this chapter, this was going to be the end of my story. Never Say Never. A second love after the suicide of your soul mate is possible. It can be beautiful in a new way. It can heal and help you grow and deepen. I wish I could have ended it here, but that was not my fate. After six years of marriage, Greg abruptly left. Once again, I felt stunned disbelief as my bubble of privilege and good fortune burst. My list of life's lessons was now adding divorce to the curriculum. Greg had been having an affair with a work colleague almost two decades his junior for over five months when he gave me a "thank you for helping me heal" note and walked out the door. As I sat at the kitchen table with my head in my hands, rereading the note and trying to grasp the unfathomable, the patio project Greg had started the prior week darkened the room. He had stacked the outdoor furniture and planters against the window, and they shaded out the fading evening light. The staging was complete for a project left unfinished.

 McKay Moore Sohlberg

Epilogue

There are moments when the world we take for granted instantaneously collapses, dissolving into incomprehensible madness. Reality topples, and the unimaginable overthrows all that seemed certain. Realizing that your spouse, whom you carefully vetted and trusted with your fragile heart cruelly deceived you is one of those moments. So is learning of a loved one's suicide. For me, the moment I learned of Olof's death is indelible and exists as an iconic, unwanted beacon of the indiscriminate nature of pain and tragedy that may lurk around the corner, and there is nothing I can do to prevent it. I imagine my daughters and others who loved Olof deeply and depended upon him for their sense of security feel similarly. Randomness trumps all. But I have learned in the decade since Olof died that my initial shattered vision of how my life would, and should, unfold is not the whole story. It's not even the most important part of my story. While it may be the most dramatic, and fraught with the most triggers, time gives the gift of perspective. The pain and shattering of dreams bear the fruit of wisdom, strength, humility, and hope and eventually give rise to new life. These are not platitudes, but hard-won truths. There is not a linear path to sunshine and roses; quite the contrary, it is winding, hilly, and often doubles back on itself. I see now that the twists and turns all serve a purpose and are part of my life journey. I know how to embrace, and even invite the dark times, while remaining open to the promise of the possibilities in the future. I realize I am resurrecting my lessons of recovery from Olof's suicide to help me with new life challenges.

Initially, Greg's infidelity and discovered betrayals were excruciatingly painful, as they ripped the bandage off the grief scab that protected my Olof wound and catapulted me back in time to those moments of disbelief when reality as I knew it was suspended. Abandonment times two. I began to realize, however, that my healing journey from Olof's suicide had changed me. Greg's departure, while similar in its abruptness and lack of warning, was not the same at all. The person writing this epilogue is not the same person who penned the early descriptions of coping after suicide. I am not the same. I have grown. I lean on the lessons I have learned as a suicide survivor.

Love doesn't end when someone dies by suicide. Olof's love was and remains a palpable, sustaining force. It grounded me as I navigated parenting and the steep learning curve of the initial years. Our foundational love helped me trust and open myself to love a new person, which I did not think would be possible. It is good to know I am capable of trust and commitment. Olof's and my shared love comforts me now when life has presented new challenges. I remember the early years when I worried that my memories of our life together might fade, or worse, that others could tarnish the memories by their misperceptions about suicide. This turned out to be needless angst. I know now that Olof will always be a positive, loving part of my life fabric.

Over the years, grief has taught me about the preciousness of life. I have felt gratitude more often and privileged entitlement less frequently. Suicide survival has taught me that I am not immune to life's tragedies, and also revealed the converse: life can still hold tremendous joy. My heart has expanded.

I also have a much different understanding of suicide. Suicide is the tenth leading cause of death in the United States. Every day more than a hundred Americans die by suicide. I had no idea. These individuals leave a cast of spouses, children, parents, siblings, friends, and colleagues all struggling to understand and move forward under the weight and complexity of suicide. This large population is caught in the shame and confusion of a mechanism of death that our culture perceives as a morally reprehensible choice, hindering an already complicated grief process. As a culture, we have not moved much to alter this false narrative. I refuse to give it credence, however, and I know I am joined by countless other suicide survivors. Writing this book has helped me find my voice. Suicide is not a willful abandonment. Despite society's confusion and biases, we know that suicide is neither an act of selfishness nor a choice. It is a result of a mind that is not well, and in many cases is an impulsive act to escape unbearable pain. The suicidal person can simultaneously feel tremendous love and also act in irrational ways. Science supports this. Sharing my journey and survival discoveries on these pages reinforces my recovery and strengthens my resolve to move the needle, even just a little, on society's understanding of suicide.

Those of us who are left behind have a hard path. We are still here. While the journey cannot be rushed and will be very different for every person—ultimately honoring our loved one means living our own life, which will continue to have triumphs and challenges. Acceptance comes first. I think this is the longest and most difficult phase. Finding a way to construct meaning by integrating the temporal triad of the past that held your loved one, with the present where their stark absence looms large, with the future where the new and beautiful, and the hard and ugly, will happen without them, is necessary to live fully. I am grateful to have had my years with Olof, and much more about our union informs and grounds me than unsettles me. I am also able to embrace a future where his suicide is not the driving force.

For me, constructing meaning through loss has been helped by using my suicide survivor voice to hopefully prevent other gun suicides. It took a long time to publicly speak about Olof's suicide: eight years to be exact. Serendipity connected me with a gun violence survivor fellowship program through the organization Everytown (everytown.org) as I was reading their information on suicide. Through their training, I learned how to use my story to advocate in small ways for sensible gun legislation, which I know could have saved Olof's life. I remind legislators or other advocacy groups that two thirds of all gun deaths are by suicide and that easy access to guns increases the risk of suicide by threefold. I share the statistics that show that firearms are the most common mechanism that allows people to *complete*, that is the term used by mental health professionals—*complete the suicide.* Had there been wait times or stricter gun laws, I remind them that my Olof might be alive today, and the world would not have lost an accomplished surgeon, a community activist, and most important to me, a gentle, adventure-filled, and very loving father and husband. For me, this little bit of advocacy has brought some solace and peace.

Finding meaning doesn't have to involve organizations or big actions. In fact, it doesn't even have to involve others.

     McKay Moore Sohlberg

Writing this book, mostly solo at my kitchen table with the fireplace aglow and the bird feeders active in the window, has brought me meaning. Putting my stories and thoughts to words has helped me process and grow. Other important recovery actions have centered around activities and rituals that bring me pleasure and joy. Being in nature with my children and friends through running, cycling, and hiking has been a literal and symbolic path to peace and wellness. I have found meaning in establishing daily self-care rituals that ground me and engender feelings of gratitude. High up on the list is my morning coffee ritual, which is the mechanism through which I greet each day that is granted to me and serves as a reminder to live that day as fully as I am able. Morning coffee time is oddly emblematic of my recovery journey; thus, I end my story by sharing the twists and turns of my daily caffeine procurement.

Morning coffee was a ritual that I learned gradually as I joined the Sohlberg clan in my early twenties. I was not one of those college students who had found caffeine-amplified study sessions useful. I had no objections to the chemicals; I just didn't like the taste. Too bitter. Olof was a regular imbiber and thoroughly enjoyed his daily "cup of joe" as he would say. His Montana family had a sweet, and very ingrained, coffee sacrament, which was how the family gathered and connected. When we visited, the coffee pot was emptied several times over as everyone hung out in various renditions of morning pjs and just talked. Initially I augmented my drink with a boatload of sugar and milk to make it palatable. It was worth tolerating the taste to enjoy the richness of family gathering. Eventually, however, I began to sincerely like my sweetened, creamy morning drink. Coffee became a morning connector for Olof and me as we married and evolved our own routines as a couple. In the later years, on Saturday after he cycled with his peloton, he would ride to our favorite Eugene coffee shop, Full City, order me my "2 percent chocolate latte" and his "double espresso" and the barista would put tape over the drinking holes and he'd ride home one-handed, coffee carrier precariously balanced, but never dropped, and deliver me my coffee. We'd begin our Saturday over coffee and share the gossip from our respective morning group exercise. After he died, I grieved the loss of my special coffee time. Each morning was a painful, searing reminder that he was gone. For many months, I battled the pain by driving myself to our coffee shop, ordering my special drink, and indulging in some therapeutic tears. I confess to being late to a number of morning meetings at the university if the coffee patron line was too long.

Eventually, I realized that the outlay of time and money for my daily obsession was not sustainable. I was lamenting my difficulty settling into daily routines without Olof to my friend Sue, and she took charge of the morning problem. She helped me pick out one of the newly available espresso makers that used prepackaged pods so I could easily make my own elegant coffee. She showed me her machine and made me a cup that was indeed delicious. I stopped clinging to what was no more, bought myself a pretty new machine, and refashioned a new home coffee routine. I reserved the coffee shop for special, sit-down events. I had learned to preserve what made sense and discard what did not.

When Greg entered the picture, he too was a coffee aficionado, and the morning coffee routine expanded and evolved to include the purchase of a fancy Swiss espresso machine. Greg took on the role of morning barista and

     McKay Moore Sohlberg

served me a carefully concocted latte with just the right amount of sugar each morning. We started almost every day over coffee. If I was running late for work, he brought it up to me in my shower. After his abrupt abandonment, the morning coffee routine once again loomed large as a painful reminder of loss. Greg owned the fancy Swiss espresso machine, and I now lacked the necessary equipment and a person who knew how to operate it, even if I still had such a machine. I found myself returning to the routine of driving to the coffee shop and ordering my Olof-blessed chocolate latte. This phase did not last long, however, as I decided I wanted to own my own upscale espresso machine and to be my own barista. I was intimidated, however, by the mechanical demands of such a machine, as I had not learned to use the espresso maker; the bells and whistles designed to provide options for making a variety of coffee drinks and to keep the machine in working order were enigmatic. But I wanted to make my own special coffee at home each morning. I reminded myself that I had evolved past the self-deprecating "I can't do anything mechanical" attitude, ignored my insecurity, located the make of the coffee machine online, and pressed "purchase."

It was six months ago that the large box containing my new Swiss espresso maker arrived. I felt proud. I committed to carefully reading the manual and uncharacteristically trying to be more detailed and systematic in my implementation of new equipment rather than engage in my usual random button-pushing trying to quickly get what I wanted. Haste makes waste. The instructions were surprisingly transparent, and my confidence rose. I filled the system with water and completed the preliminary setup. The moment of truth. Sadly, however, all I got was an unpleasant, worrisome grinding noise. Not one potable drop of coffee appeared. I tried the obvious troubleshooting actions to no avail. Defeated, I called the help line, and surprisingly someone very nice named Taylor answered. I liked that she was a she. Taylor walked me through all types of diagnostics. I felt rather techy as I successfully followed her instructions and gave feedback on what happened at each juncture. After about an hour, she sighed, "I'm sorry to have to tell you this, but your machine is defective. You've done everything right. We almost never see this." I knew that not being able to use my new high-end espresso machine was hardly a crisis, but to me it felt like a harbinger of not being able to move forward. I resisted the strong urge to overshare and explain to Taylor how important the act of independent coffee service was to my personal evolution. As if she knew, Taylor quickly told me not to worry because she would arrange for me to receive a whole new machine immediately. She explained that the new machine would be there in two days, and all I would need to do is take it out the box, replace it with the broken machine, and drop it off at the mailing company. Taylor had no idea, but her reassurance provided much more than facilitation of my morning drink. She encouraged me to troubleshoot and demonstrated that what you want might not come to fruition, but there is usually a way to manage the challenges and figure things out. Sure enough, the new machine arrived in two days, I followed the now familiar setup procedures, and voilà, yet a new morning coffee routine was born.

This past Christmas, one of my favorite gifts was a beautiful black-and-white coffee mug with the word "Nana" etched in a delicate black-and-gold scroll. I chose Nana for my name when I learned of the pending birth of my first grandchild. I immediately positioned my special mug under the spout of my spiffy espresso machine, where it is always on display declaring the joy of the future. My morning routine was enhanced once again.

As I close this book, I am just a few weeks away from becoming someone's Nana. Ericka and Lee are expecting a baby daughter. My journey, which encompasses the beautiful, the mundane, and the hard over these past ten years, is part of what I bring to the table as a daughter, mother, sister, friend, niece, aunt, colleague, and citizen. It will also be part of what I can give to the next generation. The lessons learned as a suicide survivor, as unwanted as they are, have formed me and taught me the stunning paradox of how the dark can yield the light.

Poem
Temporal Transformations

Anguish. Ache. Abhorrent.   Accept. Absolve. Ask.

Blame. Burden. Blunder.   Belief. Begin. Build.

Culpable. Confusion.   Courage. Confide. Comfort. Celebrate.

Dark. Done. Desperate.   Dare. Dodge. Dream.

Erased. Empty.   Exonerate. Entrust. Encourage.

Fatal. Foul.   Faith. Foster. Forgive. Future.

Guilt. Grief. Gone.   Grace. Give. Glimmer.

Horror.   Hope. Heal. Honor.

Irreversible. Irate.   Imagine. Incorporate. Instill.

Jarring. Jaded.   Journey. Join.

Kicked.   Kin. Kind. Kindred.

Liable. Lonely.   Liberate. Live. Love.

   McKay Moore Sohlberg

Mourn. Macabre.   Memories. Mend.

Numb. Never. Null. Nixed.   New. Noble. Nourish.

Odious.   Optimistic. Open.

Permanent. Pain. Posthumous.   Perspective. Process. Prayer. Peace.

Quaff. Quake. Quash.   Quiet. Quell.

Remorse. Regret. Reproach.   Resilience. Relinquish. Recovery. Risk.

Shame. Shock. Sadness. Scarred. Scared.   Search. Soul. Share. Sense.

Trauma. Terror.   Transcend. Talk. Touch. Tend.

Unimaginable. Unthinkable.   Understand. Unleash. Unveil.

Victim. Void.   Vow. Victory. Vanquish. Vital.

Wail. Want. Woe.   Walk. Will. Willful.

X.   XOXOXO.

Yanked.   Yes.

Zero.   Zen.

About the Author

McKay Moore Sohlberg, PhD, is a professor at the University of Oregon and author of several leading textbooks on brain injury rehabilitation. *My Empty Nest was Supposed to Have Two Birds* is her first memoir. She resides in Eugene, Oregon where in her spare time she enjoys hiking, running and cycling through Oregon's beautiful outdoors with friends and family. Her greatest joy is time spent with her three precious daughters, Ericka, Tatum, and Emma, and their exquisite partners, Lee, Jared, and Taylor. She knows that Olof would be so very proud of them.

Made in the USA
Coppell, TX
01 November 2022

85602916R00089